PRODUCTIVITY IN
SERVICE ORGANIZATIONS

PRODUCTIVITY IN SERVICE ORGANIZATIONS

Organizing for People

HERBERT HEATON, CPA, Ph.D.

Comptroller, The Rockefeller Foundation
President, Support Services Alliance, Inc.

McGRAW-HILL BOOK COMPANY
New York   St. Louis   San Francisco   Auckland   Bogotá
Düsseldorf   Johannesburg   London   Madrid   Mexico
Montreal   New Delhi   Panama   Paris   São Paulo
Singapore   Sydney   Tokyo   Toronto

Library of Congress Cataloging in Publication Data

Heaton, Herbert, date.
Productivity in service organizations.

Includes index.
1. Labor productivity.   2. Organization.
I. Title
HD57.H37   331.1'18   77-8484
ISBN 0-07-027705-2

34567890   MUBP   7865432109

The editors for this book were Robert A. Rosenbaum and Margaret Lamb,
the designer was Elliot Epstein, and the production supervisor
was Teresa F. Leaden. It was set in Palatino by J. C. Meyer & Son, Inc.

Printed by The Murray Printing Company and bound by The Book Press.

To My Extending Family

Contents

Preface

A few years ago I encountered the dictionary listing of *obnoxious* as a synonym for *responsible*. It touched off a glow of recognition and understanding like an unexpected meeting with an old friend. Then my thoughts turned back to the strange but logical trail that led to this perception. After all, the model of the world which was given to many of us as children had displayed being responsible as a virtue. It is a model I still accept and try to live by, but I am no longer surprised or hurt to find others judging me obnoxious when in all honesty, more or less, I think I am simply being responsible.

After twenty years in public accounting, I joined The Rockefeller Foundation as comptroller. A colleague described the move as dropping out—avoiding the challenge of measurable productivity under the profit system and seeking the easy life in a nonprofit organization. In the absence of acceptable measurements of productivity for nonprofit organizations, there could be no convincing rejoinder. From the first day on the job, therefore, I was looking for measurements of productivity in nonprofit organizations, and I had a unique vantage point. Only after a year or so did it dawn on me that profit-making organizations were likewise without measurements of productivity for people. The health care delivered to hospital patients is measured no better in a profit-making proprietary hospital than in a nonprofit hospital, whether public or private.

Measurements have significance in terms of their intended use. Stated conversely, results are a function of the methods and measurements used. My interest slowly became focused on only those measurements which could be used in improving the productivity of organizations. From this focus, the measurements used for descriptive and predictive purposes by economists were not relevant. Neither were measurements of performance against sliding or fixed standards such as used by teachers and cost accountants. Improving performance is a different objective from maintaining standards, and it requires different measurements.

We can maintain standards by (1) excluding below-average performers and (2) selecting only those tasks at which we excel. But are these the best methods to improve organizational productivity? Granted that they enhance the profits of organizations producing goods or selling them, and they do result in improved productivity when the measurement is output per labor hour, a measurement of people's service to organizations. But are they effective methods to meet people's needs? Are they effective methods to improve the productivity of service organizations? Obviously not. People's needs cannot be served by organizational methods which result in (1) excluding people from productive work and (2) leaving difficult tasks undone. It follows that an interest in how to improve productivity in service organizations must lead to both special measurements and special methods.

If an organization's objective is to maintain standards, then the organization must judge people and select or exclude them. As a corollary, the organization must offer opportunities and give rewards more on the basis of estimated potential than acutal performance. Colleges call for scholastic aptitude tests as a basis for admission, and the most prestigious are the most selective. Even those employers claiming merit pay systems give minor weight to work performance in determining salary increases and major weight to living costs, seniority, attitudes, and potential. In a society where what *they* think we are or will be is more important than what we do, we can live productive lives only if we learn to deflect the system's garbage.

Perhaps there is no need to change the world or change ourselves and *them*. But there is a need for changing our perceptions and the ways we act and react. Changing our perceptions is dangerous and obnoxious to the established order, but it also is an ultimate purpose of education and the starting point for changing whatever it is possible to change. Most attempts at achieving change are as temporal and ineffective as trying to move a pendulum in one direction only. By making waves, we produce social, political, and economic cycles instead of social, political, and economic progress. This book is focused on the methodology of effective change in achieving two responsible objectives: improving the productivity of organizations in serving people and developing individuals in organizations.

Mostly the book is derived from experience and observation. Associates at work helped by sharing problems and mistakes so we could learn together. My wife shared her eyes, mind, and heart, so I learned not only from her, but through her and with her. Family, friends, and strangers offered inputs beyond measure, but ultimate responsibility for the value of the book falls on its readers. Readers must contribute their own experiences to the patterns and processes set forth herein. Then the processes will be constructive only if absorbed and used.

Acknowledgments. Leo Kirschner, Henry Romney, and Chuck Pepper helped me to scrap an earlier version of this book. Five years later, Roy Fairfield, David Finks, Diane McGrary, Dermod McDermott, Gene Nameche, John Pool, and Peter Radetsky supported my decision that the time had come to start writing again. Those who read and gave feedback on the current version include Pauline Baker, Victor Baker, William Birenbaum, Frances Brancato, Margaret Farrar, Mark Gelber, George Harrar, Charles Hartmann, Olga Heaton, Harry Heinemann, Clare Howard, Robert Howard, Norman Lloyd, Ruth Lloyd, Clark Kerr, Dermod McDermott, Robert McKenna, E. T. Neumann, Rajaram Ramanathan, Henry Romney, George Peabody, Helen Petruzzi, Charles Smith, Laurence Stifel, Goodwin Watson, Carolyn Wieman, and Robert Rosenbaum's group at McGraw-Hill.

Herbert Heaton

PRODUCTIVITY IN SERVICE ORGANIZATIONS

ONE

Organization Models and the Hierarchy of Organization Methods

"Long before the peoples of the Western World turned to the machine, mechanism as an element in social life had come into existence. Before inventors created engines to take the place of men, the leaders of men had drilled and regimented multitudes of human beings: they had discovered how to reduce men to machines. The slaves and peasants who hauled the stones for the pyramids, pulling in rhythm to the crack of the whip, the slaves working in the Roman galley, each one chained to his seat and unable to perform any other motion than the limited mechanical one, the order and march and system of attack on the Macedonian phalanx—these were all machine phenomena."[1]

Two stages have been identified in the evolution of organizations: first, people have been fragmented and compartmentalized to take their specialized roles in machinelike processes, and second, the fragmented people have been displaced by machines. A third stage can now be discerned, namely, organizations respecting, using, and needing people as people.

Most of us have been brought up to believe that a dichotomy exists between efficiency and humanity—that displacement of people by machines is natural and inevitable. Our social concern has largely been focused on how idled people could use their leisure, how they could be kept off the streets and quiescent. Most of us have lived without the vision that stage three—organizations respecting and using people as people—could be practical and productive. Without the vision of stage three, without the perception model to make it visible, we have been as blind to its existence as a peasant child to the world of microbes. Stage three is our goal.

Perception, according to the *Encyclopaedia Britannica*, is the process of translating sensory stimulation into organized experience. Perception models, as we understand them, fit random personal observations into organized patterns, both cognitive and affective. This chapter offers some thoughts for interpreting organization models. Then it diagrams and discusses the Established and the Target Models for organizations and individuals. It describes the Hierarchy of Organization Methods, a powerful model from which we derive a theory of organizational change, and finally it introduces the concept of the Complete Organizational Model.

FIVE THOUGHTS FOR INTERPRETING ORGANIZATION MODELS[2]

1. From physiological psychology we learn that communication channels are one directional only. Messages from the brain to the muscles are carried on one set of nerves. Messages from the sensory receptors to the brain are carried on a different set. Interhuman communications, like intrahuman, are also carried on one-way channels. We do not hear with our mouths; nor does the head of a hierarchy receive data via the chain of command.

2. The smallest part of the human body is complete and self-sufficient. Each single cell is a complex unit that eats, digests, stores energy and burns it, tests the environment, receives stimuli, and responds. Genetically, each cell contains the whole, whatever its differentiated role in the organism. And as can be seen in the growth of a tree from the cutting of a branch, there is a capacity for changing roles. Thus it does not seem logical that superiority or inferiority are intrinsic characteristics of cells. Following this, perhaps it is not valid or useful to label messages

going down the line as orders and messages going up as passive data or information. Physiologically, the nerve impulses are apparently identical.

3. When cells accumulate and get arranged in an orderly pattern, they constitute an organ or organization. Some organs perform well, but some perform poorly and some fail. Are some cells inadequate? Poor performance may be due to poor structure—as, for example, poor vision may be related to the shape of an eyeball or lens. Poor performance may be due to atrophy arising from inactivity or improper nourishment. There may be abuse instead of use, as of a small heart in an indulgent body. The environment may be hostile, as the climate in a southern zoo for a polar bear. Without immunization and treatment, diseases can curtail and malignancies destroy. Finally, poor performance can be caused by failures in learning, coordinating, developing, adjusting, and adapting, because these must be lifelong activities like training the eye to see and the mind to perceive.

4. Feedback is basic. Infant birds hear adults of their species sing one summer and the following spring start trying to sing themselves. For several weeks they practice and listen to themselves. Starting with infantile sounds, they continually adjust toward the objective in their brains until finally they achieve it. Cover their ears and they do not adjust or achieve. In biofeedback laboratories, people given feedback on the temperature of a hand or the tension of a muscle have learned to adjust temperature and tension to the levels providing desired objectives like headache relief. Without feedback, organisms must be static and simplistic.

5. Evolution of successful organisms and organizations is a process of complexification, not simplification. The human eye has 130 million receptor cells.

Some of these receive color and others black and white; some see only objects that move across the field of vision horizontally from left to right; others see only oblique or vertical movement or movement from right to left.[3] In organisms, complexification improves durability and is a prerequisite to synergism. Simple organizations are simpleminded. With complexification, intelligence develops and self-improvement in organizational performance becomes possible. As Sir Julian Huxley wrote, "mind is generated by or in complex organizations of living matter capable of receiving information of many qualities or modalities about events both in the outer world and in itself, of synthesizing and processing that information in various organised forms, and of utilizing it to direct present and future action."[4] Tendencies toward simplification are found in the legislative process, in science, in verbal communication, and in measurement. But in organization theory we should find a tendency toward complexification.

MODELS AND THEIR PROCESSES

The Established Models

The Established Models for organizations and individuals are integrated in Figure 1-1.[5] The engendered attitudes can be recognized as those of McGregor's Theory X individual, who avoids work, does not accept responsibility, and must be directed and controlled.[6]

Communication goes one way from structure to process to attitude. Being courageous instead of fearful does not stop the system from creating failures, nor does being friendly instead of antagonistic cause the system to accept instead of reject. Cultural bias in intelligence tests, like discrimination against minorities in hiring, can and must be eliminated. But these reforms will leave unchanged the basic processes of ranking, enforcing, and rejecting and will not reach back to change the hierarchical structure.

FIGURE 1-1

The Established Perception Pattern

The attitudes are those of McGregor's Theory X individual.

STRUCTURE $\xrightarrow{\text{Legislate}}$ PROCESS $\xrightarrow{\text{Engender}}$ ATTITUDE

Hierarchy
of authority

RANK

Test	Submissive
Measure potential	Dependent
Sort and label	Conforming

ENFORCE

Prescribe	Distrustful
Supervise and police	Judgmental
Measure efficiency	Critical

REJECT

Create failures	Fearful
Strip	Helpless
Exclude	Antagonistic
	or apathetic

The place for organizational purpose in the diagram is indicated by the black dot at the peak of the hierarchical pyramid. Purpose is often introverted and personalized—to make the organization work, to be a good administrator, to run a clean, orderly school or a clean, orderly prison. The processes are mostly directed at people, not purpose. They are designed to maintain the existing order and prevent change. The attitudes they engender prevent learning.

During World War I and World War II, production goals permeated society and labor shortages forced organizations to accept whoever could be induced to apply. The result was that production boomed. It seems strange that these results were ignored or attributed to an overriding hierarchy of governmental authority which could plan, order, rank, allocate, enforce, and reject. It is not really strange, however, because our perceptions are controlled by our perception models, and alternative models were not sufficiently developed and known.

The Target Models

The Target Models for organizations and individuals are integrated in Figure 1-2. They are descriptive of current realities, not future utopias. They can be seen and observed. The engendered attitudes can be recognized as those of McGregor's Theory Y individual, who seeks to accomplish, accepts responsibility, and is self-directed, effective, and capable of learning.

Communication goes one way from structure to process to attitude, then on from attitude to another process cluster and back again to structure in a feedback loop. With feedback, purpose becomes an integral part of processes, attitudes, learning, and adapting. Purpose, in this pattern, must be organizational, not personal, and stated in terms of organizational achievement, not of internal discipline.

This pattern is more complex and less familiar. For example, here the functions of leadership are said to include absorbing hostility and making the affective cognitive. Making the affective cognitive involves learning from experience instead of vicariously, learning as an entire organism to understand, respond, and achieve instead of learning to take directives, acquire data, and

FIGURE 1-2
The Target Perception Pattern
The attitudes are those of McGregor's Theory Y individual.

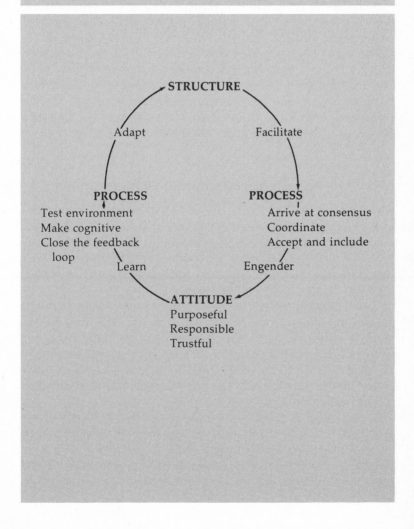

calculate objectively as if one's humanness did not exist. In the Established pattern, organization is imposed from the top down and is managed or administered. Here organization evolves in a circle and the function of leadership is to catalyze, not to impose.

How does one move toward a consensus in a conflict situation? How can a college admissions officer accept and include when there are seven applicants for every opening in the freshman class? How can standards be maintained? Is the pattern feasible only in small, select groups? Chapters 5 through 11 of this book are the "how to" part, containing instructions and illustrations for using this pattern and applying its processes at the appropriate times and in the appropriate places. How to measure organizational productivity will be discussed in this and later chapters. The measurement concepts will be used to demonstrate that the Target pattern is as necessary as the Established one.

THE HIERARCHY OF ORGANIZATION METHODS

Figure 1-3 shows the Hierarchy of Organization Methods with related organization processes. In later chapters we will discuss the Authority method of organizing and its related processes of ranking, enforcing, rejecting, and excluding. The discussion here will introduce the other methods and present the Hierarchy of Methods as a new perception model.

To begin with, the Hierarchy of Organization Methods can be viewed in relation to the human life cycle. At the Physical Force level, infants are restrained by the bars on their cribs and playpens. Then toddlers are spanked when they fail to respond to the no-no of Authority. Toilet conditioning and bribes of candy are at the Influence level; also at this level are the attempts of schools and churches to introject values, to socialize and motivate. Peer relationships involve processes at the Fusion level, and we are learning that these higher-level processes can be more powerful than the processes of Physical Force, Authority, or Influence. Finally, at the Development level there are processes of testing, cognition, and feedback which constitute the dynamics of growth and improvement.

FIGURE 1-3

The Hierarchy of Organization Methods

A basic perception model to be
used in organization development.

PHYSICAL FORCE

Manipulate
Restrain or incarcerate
Eliminate

AUTHORITY

Rank
Enforce
Reject and exclude

INFLUENCE

Connive
Condition
Introject

FUSION

Arrive at consensus
Coordinate
Accept and include

DEVELOPMENT

Test environment
Make cognitive
Close the feedback loop

Theories W, X, Y, and Z

The processes of Authority are one way and result in antagonism and apathy. They are associated with the Theory X individual, who avoids work, does not accept responsibility, and must be directed and controlled. The processes of Fusion are two way and result in consensus. They are associated with the Theory Y individual, who seeks to accomplish and is self-directed, effective, and capable of learning.

The processes of Physical Force are one way and result in *dissensus* and alienation. They are associated with what we may call the Theory W individual, who is a nonperson, an infant, or subhuman. Slaves were declared by law to be subhuman and, therefore, not protected by the Constitution. Enemies in war are perceived as savages. From personal observation, I have seen that prison inmates are perceived as Theory W subhumans.

> Not in interviews, not in weekly passages through the gates, not in walking the long corridors, not in the prison hospital, not anywhere during a semester of teaching a three-credit course in a maximum security prison did we observe a sign on the part of prison personnel of respect for the inmates or acceptance of them as humans. From the beginning we had been looking and we saw only that prison personnel serve as enforcers of the rejection process of society.

> "We get failures," said the warden. "They have failed in every way—school, church—yes, even failed in church. Most of them come from Welfare mothers. We call them Nedick kids. They are fivefold and sixfold losers before we get them.

> "For most of them, prison is a lifestyle with everything they want. They never had so much on the street. Here they have a bed, food, medical care, and dental care. Most of them had never been to a dentist outside.

> "I know the inmate mind. But now they are supposed to have rights and I can't even order one of them to work in the print shop. There is no point in teaching them to negotiate because they have nothing to negotiate with. You can't give them apple pie on sixty cents a day. Besides, they already know how to negotiate—they had plenty of practice in plea bargaining."[7]

The processes of Influence are also one way, but they require the organization to have some understanding of the individual, in this case the Theory Z individual. Theory Z individuals are not to be respected, but their weaknesses and susceptibilities are to be used to manipulate them. The conniving process covers a broad range of activities which stem from the idea that everyone has his or her price. This leads to buying, bribing, logrolling, kicking-back, contributing to campaigns, giving favors, and entertaining. These activities corrupt and degrade by focusing on the weaknesses of the Theory Z individual rather than on the merits of work or decisions.

Conditioning has been touted as the basic organizing concept,[8] the ultimate process of conforming the Theory Z individual to a social order. But can we condition the Theory Z individual to accept a good order and reject a bad one? Can we condition this individual to develop and improve in synchronization with a developing and improving organization? We cannot do so very well, because conditioning assumes the virtue of the system while at the same time it denies the value of individual judgment, virtue, and diversity.

The third major process at the Influence level is introjection. Every society socializes its young. Schools motivate, churches moralize, organizations indoctrinate, all with the aim that the young internalize the social norms. Necessary as introjection really is, it is nonetheless important that its detriments and dangers be understood. First, introjected values and attitudes are static, but values and attitudes should be dynamic, developing, and enlarging. Second, whatever is introjected is immune to experimental testing. Third, the habit of introjection leads Theory Z talkers to believe whatever they happen to say and Theory Z listeners to believe whatever they happen to hear or read. Like the other processes at the Influence level, introjection achieves its ends not on their merits but by exploiting the weaknesses and susceptibilities of individuals.

Who am I? As a wartime soldier, I am a Theory W person to our enemies, a Theory X person to my superiors, a Theory Y person to my fellow soldiers, and a Theory Z person to those who seek to indoctrinate and propagandize me. Who do I want to be? Who am I to myself? In this book, the complete person is the goal.

Some Other Correlations

In terms of transactional analysis, the Authority method correlates with parent-child transactions and Fusion with adult-adult. At the Physical Force level, transactions are parent-subhuman, or parent-thing.

At the Authority level we teach; at the Influence level we indoctrinate; at the Development level we learn. At the Physical Force level is survival; at the Authority level submission; at the Influence level loyalty; and at the Fusion level mutuality. Force and Authority correlate with defensiveness and with win-or-lose syndromes; Fusion and Development correlate with openness. At the Physical Force level we shanghai or enslave; at the Authority level we draft or conscript; at the Influence level we buy or bribe; at the Fusion level we coordinate. At the Authority level is uniformity; at the Fusion level purpose.

To arrive at consensus on the Fusion level we communicate, confront, and negotiate, but on the Authority level to confront is to be a troublemaker.

Correlation of Methods and Productivity

By Physical Force, organizations can obtain unskilled manual labor. Slaves can pull weeds and pick cotton. Shanghaied sailors can pull oars and swab decks. Prisoners can mop floors, do laundry, and work on road gangs. Forced labor must be visible to be overseen or supervised, and performance must be an obvious response to the whip or the prod. Theory W people working for survival and to avoid pain are indifferent to the goals of their masters. Socially denied, emotionally and intellectually deprived, and physically distressed, Theory W people sustain themselves with faked effort, feigned pain, and other techniques of the con.[9]

Until the Industrial Revolution, forced labor made sense economically to those who applied the force, giving them the use of multiple oars, hoes, and sledges. But reluctant labor is inefficient labor, and people cannot be beaten to use fine tools with care or machinery with efficiency. Where Physical Force continues today as a major organizing method, productivity is low. Incarceration of criminals and mental patients is expensive, and it rehabilitates or cures few. In military operations, cost effectiveness is poor, with the United States reported to have spent over $1 million per enemy soldier killed in Vietnam. To achieve efficiency, organizations look to processes at the Authority level.

At the Physical Force level we saw the individual as the beast requiring physical control. At the Authority level we find the Theory X person, acknowledged to be human but not much more. Organizations can be served only by selecting the best of Theory X people, and even those best will be lazy, lack initiative, need to be told what to do, need to be policed, and sooner or later need to be rejected and excluded. To use these flawed individuals efficiently, organizations use them not as organic wholes but as conformed parts, such as hands and backs. In Chapter 3 it will be shown that using only parts of people does not improve productivity in service organizations.

In *The Service Society and the Consumer Vanguard,* Alan Gartner and Frank Riessman[10] point out that in service activities the consumer must be a partner in the production process. A patient must give a doctor a good history if the doctor is to make a good diagnosis. The student must desire to learn and must use effective learning techniques if the teacher is to be effective. But the processes in a hierarchy of authority preclude sharing of purpose or responsibility and are essentially incompatible with partnership. The Theory X individual of the hierarchy lacks ambition, initiative, or constructive desires and is unfit for partnership. In service activities, therefore, the processes at the Authority level are nonproductive or counterproductive.

At the Influence level the consumer participates in production but is a partner only in appearance. Independent reactions are different from conditioned responses. Individual interests are different from introjected values. In the words of a professor at Columbia University's Teachers College, motivating people means getting them to do what you want them to do. So does conditioning and so does buying, bribing, and each of the other conniving processes. Partners adjust to each other, but at the Influence level it is only the individual who adjusts. And the individual is altered or adjusted to take what the organization offers. The better the Influence processes, the more the person is altered or adjusted and the less the organization responds to his or her original needs.

Like Force and Authority, Influence is useful. But its usefulness, like theirs, is transitional and limited. In a post-industrial knowledge-and-service society, both knowledge and service are restricted if controlled unilaterally by governments, schools, and other established organizations. In the last analysis, real service requires some measure of respect for those being served, but when organizations seek to influence before serving, there is disrespect. Influence exploits weaknesses instead of developing strengths.

At the Fusion level are processes which build organizations on strengths instead of weaknesses, on objectives instead of internal order. To arrive at a consensus on objectives and methods involves communication, confrontation, negotiation, and fact finding. To coordinate involves techniques of mediation and arbitration or a combination of both. To accept and include people involves, first of all, acceptance of reality. The prison official who knows the inmate mind sees stereotypes instead of real people, and if the objective is rehabilitation, the official can achieve it only symbolically. Administrative behavior at the Authority level is commonly described in terms of symbol manipulations like decision theories, information systems, and data processing. These logically result initially in symbolic achievement and symbolic cost savings like those of Robert McNamara's F-14 decision before he left the Defense Department. The gap between symbolic achievement and real achievement can be great, however, and productivity should be measured in terms of actualities, not symbols. Fusion-level processes can be productive because they deal with real people, not stereotypes and conformed parts.

To the extent our thinking is in words, we are crippled by the concept that nouns are static things. Love is not a many-splendored thing, but a many-splendored process. In complex organizations decisions are not simply events or actions but are instead processes of stating objectives and testing results in a never-ending circular flow. And only at lower levels does getting organized happen at some point in time. In complex organizations, getting organized is the continuing circular flow which was illustrated earlier in this chapter in Figure 1-2. At the top of the Hierarchy of Methods shown in Figure 1-3 is Development, which comprises a circular flow of testing, measuring, thinking, and feeding back to modify and improve performance.

Productivity also is a process, not a thing, except of course in terms of low-level, short-time-span methods with low-level, short-time-span goals. In a post-industrial knowledge-and-service society, productivity is a process and it correlates with Fusion and Development as they are integrated in the Target Perception Pattern of Figure 1-2.

Theory of Organizational Change

The nature of organizations correlates with the methods they use. And their methods change or can be made to change. As a result of changing methods, organizations change in essential nature.

Progression up the Hierarchy of Methods requires acceptance and inclusion. Regression down the Hierarchy of Methods results from rejection and exclusion. Acceptance and rejection, inclusion and exclusion, are not simple acts or decisions but are instead complex patterns of interlocking processes of which we are too little cognitive. Chapters 5, 7, 9, and 10 deal with the processes of moving organizations up the Hierarchy of Methods. At this point, we intend only to outline how progression and regression occur.

Progression. As prelude to negotiating an end to hostilities, each side must acknowledge the other and accept it as human. Otherwise Physical Force must continue as the means of seeking order, although the precise processes may shift, as from killing to enclosing in concentration camps or on reservations. When convicts are released from prison on completion of their terms, if their exclusion is continued by employment restrictions and other techniques, Physical Force remains the method of control. With acceptance, on the other hand, peace treaties can be drafted and ex-convicts employed, thereby superseding Force by Authority and a rule of law. If enemies and convicts have internalized the judgment that they are Theory W subhumans, however, acceptance and inclusion can succeed only to the extent of their concurrent changes in self-image. Such changes are not simple acts or decisions but complex patterns of interlocking processes. Chapters 6, 8, 9, and 10 deal with the processes of moving self-images up the Hierarchy of Theories.

At the Authority level, acceptance of Theory X people is incomplete. Their humanity is acknowledged, but only their parts, like hands or backs, are given a place in organizations. Acceptance of people in their entirety, but not their goals, appears at the Influence level with Theory Z people. At the Influence level organizations exploit the weaknesses and susceptibilities of people to induce them to devote their strengths to organizational goals. At the Fusion level is acceptance of Theory Y people and their goals. At the Development level there is recognition that people learn and change and there is acceptance of the complexity involved in concurrent evolution and learning on the part of both organizations and the people within them. At the Development level, infants are perceived not as Theory W subhumans but as immature Theory Y individuals.

Regression. If the tests and measurements at the Development level are used to reject and exclude people, the organizational structure becomes frozen and the consensus of the Fusion level is shattered. If the objectives of people are not fused and served by organizations, their compliance must be sought by indoctrination, conditioning, and other processes of Influence. Since all the people cannot be influenced all the time, organizations must control people by the rules of governance and chains of command which characterize hierarchies of authority.

The method of Authority is self-limiting because, as organizations reject and exclude people, these people move beyond the reach of Authority and can be dealt with only by Influence or Physical Force. As the numbers of excluded people increase, however, the Influence processes of the established order lose out to the norms of the excluded group and Physical Force becomes the establishment's method of last resort.

CONCLUSION

Within the Hierarchy of Organization Methods we have positioned both the Established Organization Model and the Target Model. Correlations were shown between methods, processes, goals, values, attitudes, and the theories or models of human behavior. The level of our methods was seen to limit the level of our accomplishments. *Accepting* and *including* were introduced not as attitudes, simple acts, or decisions, but as complex processes requiring knowledge and skill and having crucial importance to our future.

Reflection makes clear that as we move up the Hierarchy of Methods, we do not cut out the lower rungs. To develop our minds and spirits, we cannot lay waste our bodies. To achieve Fusion and Development, we cannot reject Force, Authority, and Influence. To create Target Model Organizations, we cannot renounce the Established Model. Complete Organizations encompass both models, Established and Target. Organizations that encompass only one model are either exploitive or ineffective and, therefore, of low productivity in serving people. In the next three chapters, we circle around the Established Model as it stands alone in too much of the establishment. In Chapters 5 through 8, we examine the methods and processes of the Target Model with only occasional references to the way they are built on, superimposed on, and dependent for support on the methods and processes of the Established Model. Beginning in Chapter 9, we turn to the interrelationships of methods and models in Complete Organizations and Complete Individuals.

NOTES

[1] Lewis Mumford, *Technics and Civilization,* Harcourt Brace Jovanovich, Inc., New York, 1963, p. 41.

[2] The five thoughts for interpreting organization models are extrapolated concepts rather than something directly attested to in most books or else are basic concepts which are widely known.

[3] The number of receptors in the human eye was taken from *Physiological Psychology* by Peter M. Milner, Holt, Rinehart and Winston, Inc., New York, 1970, p. 180.

[4] Sir Julian Huxley, Introduction to Teilhard de Chardin's *The Phenomenon of Man,* Harper & Row, Publishers, Incorporated, New York, 1965.

[5] Matthew P. Murgio, *Communications Graphics,* Reinhold Book Corporation, New York, 1969, was helpful in preparing charts and tables.

[6] Douglas McGregor, *Human Side of Enterprise,* McGraw-Hill Book Company, New York, 1960. Theory X and Theory Y, though now part of the language, were originally set forth in this book. Theories W and Z were

my labels for other points at which behavior can usefully be identified on the continuum through which it ranges.

[7] Material about the prison came from a private review I wrote about my experiences.

[8] B. F. Skinner, *Beyond Freedom and Dignity*, Alfred A. Knopf, Inc., New York, 1971. Conditioning as an organizing concept has been identified with B. F. Skinner.

[9] Amitai Etzioni, *Complex Organizations*, The Free Press, New York, 1961. There is a discussion of the limitations of slave labor on pages 80 and 81.

[10] Alan Gartner and Frank Riessman, *The Service Society and the Consumer Vanguard*, Harper & Row, Publishers, Incorporated, New York, 1974.

TWO

Established Models and Processes

Our heads are never empty because it is our nature to imagine when we do not know. Placed in a soundproof, lightproof, cushioned chamber, one's sensory nerves continue sporadic firing and one's mind is filled with fantasies which are indistinguishable from reality.[1] Scientists fill the unknown with hypotheses and test them. We fill our heads, from childhood on, with fantasies or assumptions about the physical and social structures around us and then these mental models shape our perceptions. Matching our environmental models, we develop self-images and then these images shape and control our self-perceptions, hopes, actions, and reactions.

Service-type organizations loom large in our environment. Born in establishment hospitals, we remain for life within the reaches of service organizations which test, rate, and place us and which control our actions by laws, behavior codes, and physical constraints. As their ultimate control, organizations wield the power to reject us, for the "gatekeepers of society" are key people in the establishment's service organizations (unions, schools, hospitals, churches, government agencies) and in big businesses. Service organizations manipulate the economy and directly control an increasing percentage of available work. While enforcing our loyalty, they concurrently assert that their own productivity in serving people is beyond measurement and above our abilities to appraise. What fantasies or assumptions do they engender as the environmental models which shape our perceptions? What matching self-images control our dreams and actions?

> The doctor reported on his trip to Vietnam: "Along one branch of the Saigon river, I saw people live, bathe, defecate and drink from the very same area outside their houses. I have a movie showing a young Vietnamese boy defecating in the Saigon river. Next to him is another little boy picking up the water for cooking that evening."[2]

On reading this report, what mental models shape our perceptions and trigger our reactions? The eye sees what the eye has means of seeing. Only those who share our models of a microscopic world and related sanitary processes can conceivably share our perceptions and react as we react.

> Referring to "educational, cultural, medical and other charitable service activities," the president emeritus of a major university testified before a congressional committee that they are almost all "labor-intensive and the opportunities for increased productivity in them are small and come slowly." His testimony was seconded by the president of a major foundation.[3]

Both were expressing an intellectual perception based on an Established Model, with substantial support from authorities using the same model. Believe them and despair! Their model of the world foresees improvement only in materialistic things; despite research in psychology and medical sciences, they seem to say our schools and hospitals will not improve. Fortunately their models are inadequate and their conclusions are wrong. It is the purpose of this book to describe more useful models with constructive processes for improvement and development in service organizations.

THE ESTABLISHED ORGANIZATIONAL MODEL: HIERARCHY OF AUTHORITY

The Established Model for getting organized is to create a hierarchy, that is, to classify people by position or rank with each position subordinate to the one above it. Historical examples of the hierarchical organization include families, churches, plantations, and armies. Current examples include government bureaucracies, which fit their workers into as many as fifteen civil service grades, and schools, which rank their students by percentiles of aptitude. An implicit assumption is that this is the way to get the work and learning done.

Organization manuals define the hierarchy in terms of titles, pay grades, and job descriptions, with each ranked against the others, above or below, superior or inferior. When people are admitted to organizations, they are appraised and rated. Then they are assigned the organization's title, pay grades, and job descriptions, and for organization purposes each is ranked against the others, above or below, superior or inferior. Within the organization, inferiors are referred to collectively as hands, troops, slaves, and children, boys or girls. Superiors are referred to as parents, supervisors, and bosses, or simply and directly as superiors. For organization purposes, inferiors are directed, supervised, checked up on, rewarded, punished, indoctrinated, motivated, and kept in place by superiors. In other words, each person in an organization comes close to being viewed, treated, and forced to act in toto as a person in accordance with his rank in the hierarchy, above or below, superior or inferior.

Authority

Of course it would be ridiculous for inferiors to tell superiors what to do and where to go. Therefore, organizations endow superiors with authority to make decisions, establish objectives, ordain order and uniformity, formulate rules, and force inferiors to conform and comply. Without such authority there is, by dictionary definition, a state of anarchy, with disorder and confusion. When the United States Supreme Court ruled that teachers could work until the last few weeks of pregnancy if they wished and were able, Justice William H. Rehnquist dissented. Emphasis on individualized treatment for teachers is, he said, "in the last analysis nothing less than an attack upon the very notion of law-making itself."[4]

Although organizational rules may directly apply only to organizational positions and behavior, in fact they extend as far as the organization can reach or see. Police officers and foundation officers are among those who are told they cannot moonlight without permission. In social activities, the families of military officers may be assigned the officers' positions in the hierarchy. Symbols of organizational status are worn in public and given public recognition. Even a casual observer at traffic court, night court, or a parent-teachers meeting can see status symbols recognized and reacted to with differences in treatment. These status symbols are also used to appraise the value of accomplishments at work or in school and to judge the appropriateness of aspirations.

When authority is not accepted by those over whom it is exercised, it is known as tyranny. When it is accepted, authority is considered legitimate. Lack of acceptance is indicated by attempts to move out of one's place in the hierarchy; acceptance is indicated by staying in place. A variety of techniques have been used by organizations to get people to stay in place and thereby maintain the legitimacy of the organizations' authority. The armed services have kicked out those who stepped out of line.[5] Commercial companies have exacted forfeiture of the accrued pension benefits of those who left prematurely. Unions have advanced the concept of seniority, thereby assuming the virtue of keeping workers in their place. Of necessity, for every organizational technique of control that is outlawed, another is attempted to take its place.

Transactional analysis is a relatively new way of understanding behavior.[6] As the first analytic step, each party to a transaction is identified as acting in one of three possible roles—parent, adult, or child. In a hierarchy, transactions between a superior and subordinate are parent to child and reciprocally child to parent. Someone in the middle of a hierarchy acts as a child to a superior or parent, then turns around to act as parent to a subordinate or child. So pervasive is the hierarchical model in homes, schools, and at work that many people never have a chance to learn the adult role or to function in it.

Patterns of attributes are associated with each role. The parent is directive, critical, and judgmental. The adult is observant, responsible, and coordinate. The child is uninformed, incapable of sound decisions, and irresponsible. The parent speaks and the child listens and accepts. The subordinate who responds to a directive by calling attention to certain facts that make it inappropriate is responding adult to adult instead of child to parent. Creating a crossed transaction by responding adult to adult quite obviously means stepping out of place in the hierarchy and is quickly repressed, seldom repeated. Usually the crossed transaction is impossible, because information is withheld from subordinates which would enable them to respond as adults. In other words, hierarchical organizations require subordinates to assume the attributes of subordinates—or in the language of transactional analysis, of children. Racial and occupational stereotypes are thus seen to be created and enforced by the system and not to be intrinsic characteristics of people.

Responsibility and Morality

From the viewpoint of hierarchical organizations, obedience and compliance are essential responses to authority, and therefore they are defined as virtues in people. The "good" students learn what they are told and the "good" children or subordinates do what they are told. Psychologists describe obedience and compliance as conditioned responses which can be obtained from animals and children by carefully designed programs of reward and punishment. It is important to understand that organizations seek to obtain the conditioned responses which they define as virtues. It is also important to understand that hierarchical organizations seek to exclude the virtues which they cannot condition, such as adult responsibility and morality.

Authority and responsibility move in opposite directions. Tell me what I must do and you become responsible for the results of my actions. As directives move down the line of command, responsibility moves up, becomes diffused, and vanishes. Being responsible means being accountable for something within one's power or control. It is personal and direct, not remote and abstract. When a commander-in-chief accepts personal responsibility for all acts of all subordinates, we are being conned. The only punishment will be inflicted on somebody down the line who can't prove he or she was following orders.

There are stages in the development of moral values just as there are stages in all other aspects of growth and development. The child, as the role is demanded of subordinates and defined by transactional analysis, is too immature to enable morality to determine behavior. It is appropriate, therefore, for organizations to find that subordinates cannot be counted on to be trustworthy, conscientious, and reliable. In consequence, not only must they be told what to do, but their actions must be closely supervised and controlled.

To the extent that control is exercised, responsibility and morality are excluded. Control is exercised over obedience and compliance; sins and errors of commission in carrying out orders are recognized and dealt with. Sins and errors of omission, when important actions are not ordered, are not recognized or dealt with. When subordinates perceive sins and errors, successes and failures in organizational terms, they have become part of the system. They have been conditioned to behave as compliant children without responsibility and morality.

Workers with special knowledge, like lawyers, actuaries, and tax accountants, are threats to the hierarchy. Speaking with the authority of their special knowledge, they must speak as responsible and observant adults. When given parent-to-child directives, they are unable to respond child to parent without giving up their specialty. It is hard to tell a tax accountant what to do unless you are a tax accountant yourself.

Organizations meet this problem by excluding those with special knowledge from any place in the hierarchy. These people are clustered like satellites around a superior, given titles such as consultant or staff, and denied authority or responsibility except to influence and advise the superior around whom their careers revolve. In a hierarchy, those who have any special knowledge not possessed by their superior will either be placed in a staff position or have the importance of their knowledge denied. Denial is the routine process.

Learning and Work

It is becoming harder and harder for individuals to learn or to work on their own. Formal education is compulsory and apprenticeships have dwindled away. Individual craftwork has been moved into factories; individual medical practice has been moved into clinics or hospitals; family farms have been taken over by agribusiness corporations. When learning and work are taken over by hierarchical organizations, they are sliced into tasks or jobs. The organization then decides how the tasks or jobs are to be performed and who will perform them. In other words, planning is separated from doing; it follows that without special provision for feedback and adjustment, a static, unimproving pattern of operation is established.

In this pattern, the organization needs measurements to determine a fair day's work or a fair day's scholastic achievement. This involves detailed instructions, procedures, and standards on such matters as shovel size and shovelfuls per hour or word size and spelling words per lesson. Against time, performance in work or learning is defined by the organization as up to or below its standards, and the worker or student is labeled as successful or failing.

The levels in a hierarchy can now be described. At the lowest level are people—the workers or students who actually accomplish whatever is supposed to be done. Above them are the teachers, police, and other front-line supervisors who have daily contact with the people. Telling the supervisors what to force or entice the people to do are the technicians and curriculum specialists who write procedures, and the bureaucrats who write rules and regulations. Above them are decision makers and planners who possess expertise and credentials in management or educational sciences and theories. Above them are trustees or board members who set policies.

Policy has to emerge from practice, however, or it is merely a figment of the imagination. It should not be surprising, therefore, that a major study of how trustees actually function concludes that they do not establish policies.[7] Following down the line, decision making and planning are processes which evolve from reflection about experience. It should not be surprising, therefore, that there are those who believe hierarchical planning and decision making can succeed only in mythology, that the total planning and control in a communist state can not match free enterprise and rugged individualism. Next down the line, it can be observed that most laws, regulations, and rules are honored in the breach. Finally it can be observed that teachers cannot force or entice students to learn, supervisors cannot force assembly-line workers to tighten nuts with consistent perfection, and guards cannot run a prison. Students, workers, and inmates effectively control many of their own activities in terms of their own rules, plans, policies, and objectives.

Getting something done is rarely the top priority in a hierarchy, and sometimes it is not even a major objective. In classrooms, discipline takes precedence over learning. In politics, getting reelected takes precedence over service. Negative goals like avoiding mistakes, criticism, and trouble take precedence over positive goals. As analyzed by Berne,[8] organizational resources are assigned first to defending the organization's external boundaries and second to maintaining its internal structure; only residual resources are assigned to work. In other words, the priorities of the hierarchy are to maintain the hierarchy.

The Basic Process

The basic process of a hierarchy is to convert work problems into people problems. The first step is to be selective in admitting or hiring, and the more selective an institution, the higher its prestige. Being selective usually involves the parallel process of being exclusive—excluding those who deviate from the institution's normal standards or patterns. The assumption is that an institution's standards for accepting and its patterns for excluding are valid criteria for admitting students or hiring workers. The process is to judge human worth and potential.

When a work error occurs, the first question is not why, but who is to blame. Inexorably the blame is laid on someone at the bottom of the hierarchy. The front-line supervisor says, "What can you expect from the kind of people we get these days?" The technician who wrote the procedure says, "You can't cover every little detail; you have to leave something to common sense and initiative." The inspector or auditor says, "Too bad, but I can't check everything." The process is scapegoating. Then when the punishment is meted out, there is usually some reason to say, "Don't waste your sympathy, he brought it on himself." Up and down the hierarchy, the work error is unanimously converted into a people problem.

After hiring people, personnel departments may ask for an annual review of the strengths and weaknesses of each employee. Forms call for ratings on such traits as punctuality, tact, cooperation, initiative, potential for leadership, and even loyalty. On the other hand, the forms seldom call for any details about the quality and quantity of the employee's work. The evaluation model is to judge people instead of performance.

In elite nonprofit organizations, the evaluation model tends to be elitism. Two lines of argument are involved. First, since the organizations have selected the best people, evaluation of performance is irrelevant. After all, if the best people could not succeed, who could do better? Second, since the quality of the organizations and their output is determined primarily by the quality of their people, attention to system, methods, or management is inconsequential. It follows that, if the organizations already have the best people, "the opportunities for increased productivity in them are small and come slowly." Finally, it should be noted that elitism tends to create self-perpetuating closed circles whose members are exempt from review except by peers within.

Converting work problems into people problems is a process of denying organizational accountability. It is a process of establishing a hierarchy of special privilege and immunity to rank with the hierarchy of authority. It is a process of maintaining the status quo; it denies both the need for change and the possibility.

THE ESTABLISHED INDIVIDUAL MODEL: CONFORMED PARTS

Our models are patterned filters through which we interact with the world and with each other. What we see and hear, do and say, that is consistent with our models moves through for processing; what is inconsistent is screened out. Patterns of interactions between people who share Established Models tend to confirm the models, but when models are disparate, the transactions are crossed, reactions are screened out, and communications are broken. We never see or feel everything, and our presence is never fully seen or felt by others. When we speak and act, we are acknowledged, like Ellison's black Invisible Man,[9] only to the degree that we pass through the models that others impose on us.

The pervasive Established Model for the individual is that imposed by Established Model Organizations as the complement to the hierarchy of authority. With work sliced into tasks and jobs, organizations see only parts of people—hands for manual labor, brains for planning, eyes and ears for auditing, personalities for selling. People's parts are seen as pegs to fill organizational slots—square pegs for square holes, round or oval pegs for round or oval holes. If the fit is wrong, the burden is on the individual to change. As they say in the army, "Shape up, get with the system."

Helplessness

Oppression is the state of being weighed down, subjugated, or overwhelmed by authority. Experienced subjectively and emotionally, it is known as helplessness. Patterns of personal adaptations to oppression and feelings of helplessness have been diagrammed by Seymour Halleck.[10] He identifies four methods of adaptation: conformity, activism, criminality, and mental illness. Most of us have several methods in our repertoire.

Conformity. Conformity is the method of personal adaptation which consists of accepting oppression and helplessness and making the best of them. It is the most common method, and it involves not only obedience to authority but also emotional acceptance of hierarchical rewards and punishments. Conformists, having surrendered to an organization, become apathetic when it does not motivate them. They require, for example, that teaching be subordinated to entertaining them, holding their attention, or disciplining them. They opt to be passive, decline initiative, and become spectators instead of participants; these are normal reactions to being rewarded for doing what one is told, being punished for acting independently, and being made a sucker of for doing something voluntarily.

Superficially it might appear that conformity would concentrate in the lower ranks of a hierarchy and decrease as one scans upward toward the peak of the pyramid. A moment's reflection will show, however, that it is the officer graduate of the military academy who epitomizes the military system, not the lowly draftee. Similarly it is the person on the way up that William H. Whyte described in *The Organization Man*,[11] not the messenger or typist. Helplessness moves up the ladder too. Constraints on planning and decision making envelop most executives. Their problems of leadership seem solvable only by providing greater rewards and greater punishments where lesser ones have failed.

Conformity involves acceptance of humiliation and silent internal suffering. As Saul Gellerman observed in connection with "frozen" groups, "A shred of self-respect is preserved by denying that the individual really counts for anything or that achievement is anything more than an illusion." The basic attitude is, "Let those who have privileges worry about responsibility; trust only the man who is as lost and defeated as you are; shun the man who hasn't given up the struggle for the fool will only make life harder for the rest of us."[12] Pride emerges from identification with the organization instead of from personal achievement. Criticism of the organization becomes unbearable, as evidenced by slogans such as "My country right or wrong" and "Love it or leave it."

Activism. Activists attempt to change the system by criticism, protest, and pressure. As a personal adaptation to oppression, activism has one disadvantage—it brings the whole world down on the activists' heads. Organizations rush to counterattack, smother, and smear them because the first priority is to defend the external and internal boundaries which shape the system. Conformists rush to counterattack, condemn, and abuse because activists threaten not just the system but the conformists' shred of self-esteem. The establishment and its leaders strangely and emotionally combine with victims and conformists to destroy or exclude the activists who assert the need for change.

Criminality and Mental Illness. Criminality is another adaptation to oppression and helplessness, and it can be viewed as necessary and constructive. Without it, neither individuals nor organizations can function effectively.

A crime is a violation of law, rule, or regulation. But there are too many rules. When railroad employees, air traffic controllers, and fire fighters have followed their rule books during job actions, few trains have run, few planes have flown, and fire engines have given delayed responses. If anything is to get done in daily life, we must selectively break the rules. *Red tape* is our term for rules and regulations which impede effective action, and we scorn the officious person who meticulously follows bureaucratic rules. But when there is an accident or complaint, no distinction is made between good crimes and bad. Practicality and achievement are irrelevant, and the verdict is only whether or not there has been some violation of law, rule, or regulation. We are all criminals except perhaps the bureaucrat, and we have all developed our defenses against being caught.

A police officer on patrol duty has an impossible task, the evenhanded enforcement of all laws and regulations without differentiation or priority. What can a police officer do when the delivery and shipment of goods for an important business on the beat requires the illegal parking of trucks? Business must go on, and the officer who interferes knows the heavens will descend. The question is how to safely ignore the trucks yet ticket illegally parked cars down the block. Accepting a gratuity from the business is a solution. By sharing the payment with a superior, the police officer buys protection from outside criticism or complaint. Law enforcement becomes enforcement of hierarchical position and privilege, and there is no higher legitimacy in a hierarchy. What we call police corruption is seen, from this point of view, to be an adaptation by police to oppression and helplessness in performing their assigned tasks by responding to the realities of hierarchical status and power.

Mental illness is an adaptation that does not conform to hierarchical status. In Halleck's words, psychotic behavior is like criminality except that it appears unreasonable.[13] Nameche has described some psychoses as ideas which are out of era and out of place.[14] Thus corruption and criminality appear to be normal reactions or adaptations, whereas mental illness and psychotic behavior appear to be unreasonable reactions or adaptations. Violence, whether it appears reasonable or unreasonable, whether it is legitimate, criminal, or psychotic, is an extreme adaptation to helplessness and an inability to cope.[15]

Day by day and hour by hour we vary our adaptations. We double park, stretch deductions on our tax returns, and cheat on exams. We yell at our children or subordinates and rage sullenly against unjust demands of our superiors. We use the big lie to get compliance and the big whine to get rewards. Then we conform except for sporadic forays into activism like writing to our legislators or attending a protest meeting at our children's school.

Learning and Work

A primary function of schools is socialization or preparation of students for their roles in life. Regardless of how they start, children soon conform to the stereotypes which the hierarchy imposes on them.

Formal education is mostly training in repetition. In the Established Model, the student, by reciprocity, becomes a mimic, copycat, imitator, plagiarist, simulator, reproducer, and repeater. Lesson plans define what a student is to reproduce, and uniform examinations rank performance against fellow students. The role of the student as he or she seems to act it out in the hierarchical group processes of formal education is not to grow and develop but to find a place and stay in it.

The student is defined by the school as child, not adult. Observation and inductive reasoning are adult attributes, so we should not be surprised to find them denied the child and excluded from formal education. This is especially true because observation and inductive reasoning are mechanisms of change and personal growth. Even laboratory classes are structured to confirm textbook information rather than to foster experimentation and the development of observational and reasoning skills. Faced with the unknown on a test, students complain that the material wasn't covered in class, thereby confirming themselves as merely the conformed reciprocal of the system.

Outside school the unknown remains unknown and unseen. Well-educated lawyers, accountants, and executives obtain their information mostly from the words they read in reports, cases, statistical summaries, newspapers, and trade journals or words they hear in meetings and in conversations with friends and associates. They reason and act by manipulating words, but lacking firsthand observation and inductive reasoning, their roles are scarcely more complete than those of assembly-line workers. Only rarely does one find a complete person instead of a conformed part in a hierarchy.

Apprenticed to a Yacqui Indian sorcerer, Carlos Castaneda[16] found he was learning philosophy and raising his level of consciousness. The second enemy to becoming a man of knowledge, he was told, is clarity. The sources of clarity in this sense are oversimplification, a limited field of view, a limited perspective, and a one-dimensional approach. All sources are provided by the hierarchy. The schools provide neatly encapsulated lessons and courses. Hospitals and government agencies slice work into precisely defined repetitive tasks. Workers in factories and offices are arrayed to perform small, simplified tasks in sequence. The hierarchy welcomes clarity as a friend and as a consequence expects perfection. Lawyers, accountants, and executives achieve their perfection by the elegant manipulation of words and symbols which is their task, their field, and their level of consciousness.

The Basic Process

The basic process of an individual in a hierarchy is to avoid mistakes. In school and on the job, individuals are rated by their errors, for their tasks are predetermined. There is no premium for achievement outside assigned hierarchical tasks, but there are penalties for every shortfall from perfection.

The normal distribution in a hierarchy includes a percentage of failures, so grading on a curve means that students making the most mistakes are given failing grades. If the failing students learn and improve fully as fast as their peers, they still must fail because their relative position on the grading curve remains the same. Thus they are taught passivity and place within the hierarchy. When failing students are eliminated, those next above them succeed to the failing category. The rule of thumb is for one-third to leave between the fifth and twelfth grades, mostly from the bottom ranks. The next third become failure-threatened, declining in rank regardless of effort or improvement. Apprehension then blocks learning so there can only be unskilled repetition. Thus this middle third is taught submission and place within the hierarchy.[17]

Students in the top third are neither failing nor failure-threatened, so they can actively avoid mistakes and their consequences. They can sometimes risk learning because before they are graded they have margin to absorb and time to correct the mistakes which are a part of learning. They can cheat with little risk because cheating to maintain order and hierarchical status is winked at, while cheating at the bottom to avoid penalties and place is dealt with sternly. They can be realistic in their aspirations, while the failure-threatened must seek easy tasks or take long shots where failure cannot be held against them.

It should be noted that the concept of making a mistake or giving a wrong answer is not intrinsic. When infants learn to walk they view each step as a success unless society defines each fall as a mistake and inflicts penalties for clumsiness and failing. When a student answers, "Yes, the sun rises in the east," the context of the question and the levels of the questioner and grader determine whether the answer is deemed right or wrong. The expected answer might be, "No, the earth rotates and the sun does not rise." In any event, the way to improve individual performance is by learning, not by conforming to judgments, grades, and places as set by hierarchical superiors and not by trying to avoid what they call mistakes.

To avoid mistakes is a process of constricting consciousness and foregoing learning. It is a process of accepting place and fate and status quo; it means personal sublimation to the established privilege of a hierarchy of authority.

CONCLUSION

It requires movement for us to see, and our models are invisible if we leave them at rest. It requires pressure for us to feel, and the forces which drive our models and bind them together will be unfelt if we conform and drift with their currents. The models in this chapter are for conjecture and interpretation, experimentation and manipulation.

NOTES

[1] Peter Milner, *Physiological Psychology,* Holt, Rinehart and Winston, Inc., New York, 1970. The idea that neurons fire spontaneously appears, among other places, in this book. Experimentation in sensory deprivation is from Life Science Library, *The Mind,* by John Rowan Wilson and the Editors of Time-Life Books, New York, 1969.

[2] John H. Knowles, M.D., "Health in Vietnam and Urban America," Occasional Paper No. 3, The Education Research Center, The Massachusetts Institute of Technology, Cambridge, 1968.

[3] Dr. Robert F. Goheen, former President of Princeton University and Chairman and Chief Executive Officer of the Council on Foundations, testified before the Senate Subcommittee on Foundations on October 1, 1973, on the low potential for productivity improvement in nonprofit organizations. His support came from Dr. Russell G. Mawby, President of the Kellogg Foundation, on October 2, 1973.

[4] *New York Times*, Jan. 22, 1974.

[5] *New York Post*, Mar. 20, 1974. The idea of military coding of discharge papers has received occasional newspaper publicity. A recent citation is an article in this issue of the *Post* which states, "The Pentagon records obtained by the Congressmen show that last fiscal year 35,640 servicemen discharged under honorable conditions, receiving both honorable and general discharges, got adverse SPN numbers."

[6] Thomas A. Harris, *I'm O.K., You're O.K.*, Harper & Row Publishers, Incorporated, New York, 1969. Transactional analysis is described in a number of books. This is, perhaps, the best known.

[7] Myles L. Mace, *Directors: Myth and Reality*, Harvard Business School, Cambridge, 1971.

[8] Eric Berne, M.D., *The Structure and Dynamics of Organizations and Groups*, Grove Press, Inc., New York, 1963.

[9] Ralph Ellison, *The Invisible Man*, Random House, Inc., New York, 1951.

[10] Seymour Halleck, *Psychiatry and the Dilemmas of Crime*, Harper & Row, Publishers, Incorporated, New York, 1967.

[11] William H. Whyte, Jr., *The Organization Man*, Simon & Schuster, Inc., New York, 1956.

[12] Saul W. Gellerman, *Motivation and Productivity*, American Management Association, New York, 1963. Page 60 of this book is the source of the quotation dealing with helplessness. Gellerman's Chapter 4, called "Further Harvard Studies," has a description of "frozen" or "sick" groups which is important to anyone interested in organizational change. Another quotation from page 58 of Gellerman's book reads, "Although they are seemingly self-defeating, there is an underlying logic to frozen groups. They protect the member from being isolated from his fellow workers. Fear of isolation was so powerful a force in the workers studied that it overrode all the other motives they may have had, including even the desire for self-development."

[13] Halleck, op. cit., pp. 46–47.

[14] Gene Nameche, in personal conversation.

[15] Rollo May, *Power and Innocence,* W. W. Norton & Company, Inc., New York, 1972.

[16] Carlos Castaneda, *The Teachings of Don Juan,* Ballantine Books, Inc., New York, 1971.

[17] Arthur Koestler, *The Roots of Coincidence,* Random House, Inc., New York, 1972. The relationship of sublimation and passivity appears on pages 118 and 119 of this book. Chapter 2 was recommended to me by Dr. Roy Fairfield as an excellent discussion of how mental models can confine and restrict perception and thinking. My description of models in this book does not draw on Koestler, but gains confidence from him. This can also be said of material on computer models in *Industrial Dynamics* by J. W. Forrester, The MIT Press, Cambridge, 1961.

THREE

Taking the Measure of Established Model Organizations

Measurement is a means of control and manipulation. Land is surveyed to tax and convey it. Carpets and curtains are measured for cutting to fit floors and windows. Average daily balances, shares owned, and market values are measured to pay interest and dividends or to calculate return on investment. Distance is measured to aim weapons, charge for plane tickets, and estimate travel time. Time is measured to schedule work, study, play, confinement, and the enforced start of retirement. Measurement is purposeful, not neutral; shaped by social structure, not independent; distorted by intellectual conventions, not unbiased.

Established Model Organizations measure people in order to control and manipulate them to serve organizational needs. Colleges and businesses measure applicants to see if they have potentials to fit in. Courts measure offenders to see if they are willing and able to conform to society's behavioral norms. License bureaus measure people to see if they are up to standards for cutting hair, driving taxis, or practicing accounting. Meat, eggs, and people are graded for the benefit of those who use them.

Things that are not measured are not controlled. By not measuring the productivity of organizations in serving people, we have relinquished control over organizations. By letting organizations measure us, we have given them power to control us, power which is free from effective limitation or responsibility, power which organizations can and do use to manipulate us and, if we do not meet their needs, to destroy us.

CONVENTIONAL MEASUREMENTS:
PRODUCTIVITY OF PEOPLE FOR ORGANIZATIONS

Accountants measure elements of organizational profits quite well, but they ignore costs like pollution and depletion of limited resources which do not affect profits because they are dumped on people. The production of goods and services for people are among the ostensible objectives of organizations, but neither financial accountants nor cost accountants measure productivity for people. Instead, accountants assume what we know to be false—that every dollar of organizational revenue or profits represents values delivered or values added.

When economists measure gross national product, they use input as the measure of service output and assume that every dollar spent on health care or education in a given place in one year yields the same return as a dollar spent anywhere else in any other year. In other words economists, like accountants, assume the very thing that must be measured and controlled—organizational productivity for people.

Engineers originated our conventional ideas of productivity measurement. Dating from Frederick Taylor and other pioneers in scientific management and based in part on time-and-motion studies, productivity measurement involves engineered standards of performance and narrowly focused concepts of efficiency. Usually expressed in terms of physical quantities of production per worker, these conventional productivity measurements are "laid on" people, not on organizations. They are measurements of the productivity of people in serving organizations. Measurements that are used by the system are part of the system.

Examples of Conventional Measures

Where output is easy to measure, New York City develops productivity indexes—such as tons of refuse collected per sanitation truck shift.[1] The federal government develops productivity indexes such as the number of checks and bonds issued per employee year by the Bureau of Accounts of the Treasury Department.[2] The federal government also compares actual output with predetermined standards, such as standards for the number of pieces of first-class mail to be processed per hour in post offices.

Increasing productivity in terms of such measurements, however, invariably reduces organizational service to people. Less frequent garbage pickups means more pickup weight per stop and per truck shift, but less sanitation. More checks per hour means reduced services in handling exceptions and correcting errors. More pieces of mail per hour means eliminating the distinction between first-class and airmail without regard to the utility of that distinction for the people who use the postal service.

Output of surgeons has been measured in terms of "hernia-equivalents."[3] This may be a good measurement of a surgeon's efficiency in keeping a hospital's operating room busy, but it also encourages unnecessary operations, which now number one in four or one in three. Statistics are kept for traffic tickets issued by police officers and for additional taxes assessed by tax examiners, and these statistics may be compared with defined or implied quotas. Obviously it is quicker to issue tickets for routine traffic violations such as failing to come to a full stop at a stop sign than it is for serious offenses such as reckless or drunken driving. Therefore, ticket quotas lead to petty harassment rather than real service to people and improvement in highway safety. Quotas for additional assessments by tax examiners encourage taxpayers to put something in their returns for the examiners to throw out.

Where output is difficult to measure, attention shifts to the processes of assigning work to facilities and people. For example, in reviewing medical care, utilization studies are common. These include comparing the length of actual hospitalizations with standards for the conditions being treated. Also the incidence of illness in a community is measured and compared with the incidence of treatment. Public accountants review a client's system of internal control and compare it with predetermined standards; emphasis is on measuring division of organizational duties rather than on what is accomplished.

Where processes are difficult to standardize, organizational resources are measured. Accreditation of a college, for example, depends on meeting minimum standards for faculty-student ratio and for the number of books in the library. But who, what, why, when, and how are the important questions if a college is to serve people. Hospitals are expected to maintain predetermined staff-patient ratios. But efficient operations are a poor substitute for disease prevention. The federal government forecasts personnel requirements "based on statistical data in respect to workload, activity rates, peakload requirements, safety standards, etc." An example is the staffing of air traffic control towers "based on peak-hour traffic and human stress factors." But standard staffing is of little value in serving people if small private planes absorb the facilities and efforts intended for large public jet planes. Measurements of resources and their allocation are the bases for budgetary controls over spending and the use of equipment, not for determining and controlling the services that organizations provide to people.

In profit-making companies, budgets are intended to control costs and profits. In nonprofit organizations, budgets are authorizations to incur costs without measurement of results to be achieved. The budgeting process in nonprofit organizations follows Robinson's law: organizational needs expand to consume available funds.[4] Old activities continue as long as funding continues. Budgeting in nonprofit organizations is incremental, and organizational development is opportunistic—new activities are added as defined by new funding sources. Productivity for people is not a consequence of such budget processes.

Objectives and Methods

In Established Organizations, measurements control objectives and methods. College professors who are rated by their publications devote more time to research and less to teaching, more time to writing and less to student conferences. If the measurement of a school or teacher is student performance on a statewide examination, contents of courses tend to be defined by test areas and methods of teaching tend to include drill in prior years' examinations, in anticipated questions for the current year, and even in actual questions for the current year if these become known in advance.

> There is the story of a Russian nail factory. Given a quota which was measured in tons of nails produced, the factory produced only railroad spikes. When the measurement was changed to number of nails produced, the factory shifted to producing tacks and brads. Neither measurement, of course, expressed the objective of a balanced output.

If medical research is to be funded in proportion to the seriousness of medical ailments, then allocations and objectives will depend on what standard of seriousness is applied—death, disability, hospitalization, or workdays lost.

It seems to be the nature of managers and intellectuals to criticize and deprecate. One technique is to distort history by the retroactive application of a conventional productivity measurement to some great achievement. For example, the Green Revolution has been criticized for focusing on increases in yield per acre. As a result, the criticism goes, the intensive use of insecticides and fertilizers caused dangerous pollution, and the intensive use of mechanical equipment increased fuel consumption beyond the ability of the world to sustain. In fact, however, the goals were not stated in terms of yield per acre. The record appears in *Strategy toward the Conquest of Hunger* by J. George Harrar.[5] Over twenty years ago, Harrar was stressing the needs for developing nonpolluting solar energy, breeding disease resistance into grain crops, farming the sea, developing technologies of synthetic photosynthesis, developing methods of population control, facing long-range problems as well as short-range, changing agricultural education, and changing tradition, attitudes, and perceptions throughout the world. Great goals and great achievements cannot be encompassed in small, conventional measurements of productivity.

Standards and Values

A standard is what authority says ought to be. For example, schools, prisons, and armed services commonly have standards for length of hair and type of apparel. Perhaps the ultimate standard of appearance is exact uniformity. Wearing of uniforms is associated mostly with nonprofit hierarchies of authority—hospitals, schools, churches, armed services, police departments, fire departments, sanitation departments, youth brigades, and even citizens at large in some countries. Any failure to conform to standards of appearance is commonly perceived as a defiance of authority and a rejection of social values.

Standards of behavior are how authorities say people ought to act. When failure to conform can be measured, punishment or expulsion may ensue. For example, most organizations expect employees to report to work on time and to avoid extensive personal use of the telephone. Lateness is easy to measure, but personal use of the phone in an office is not. Measurements of lateness are used to dock pay and justify firing, but personal use of the phone is rarely timed and, therefore, rarely acted on. Since authority loses potency without measurements, hierarchies of authority lose effectiveness in areas and at levels where measurements are absent or inadequate. Compulsively, hierarchies sustain their authority, but not their effectiveness, by asserting surrogate measurements; lateness is treated as a surrogate for attentiveness in general and thus as an indirect measure of daydreaming, time in the restroom, time spent using the phone on personal business, et cetera. The speciousness of surrogate measures is well known.[6]

Work output standards are part of a control system. At their worst, output standards are piece rates which exploit migrant farm workers. At their best, output standards fairly and clearly define the tasks of workers so nothing is required but following orders and working hard. The better the standards, the better the definition of the organizational tasks and slots, the more obvious it is that workers are only conformed parts. In an article on productivity management, David Sirota observes that engineered standards "have a self-defeating quality; in the long run they discourage precisely what they are designed to encourage—namely, higher worker productivity."[7] Buying the part and disrespecting the whole person is a peculiar way to provide incentives and motivation.

> In a toy factory, a team of women sprayed paint on toys moving steadily along a carefully paced assembly line. A psychologist persuaded management to let the workers try regulating the speed of this moving belt to fit their preferred pace. The workers were paid on a piece-work basis. They liked the innovation because they could speed up when their energy was high and slow down when they tired. The engineers were appalled by the irregular rates, but increasing output silenced their objections. Before long, production on this worker-regulated assembly line rose to uncomfortable heights. Workers in this department were taking home more pay than were supervisors in other parts of the factory. To cut

their piece-rate would, of course, have demoralized these workers. Finally, despite the less efficient production, the uniform flow of work had to be resumed. Too much efficiency in one subsystem proved too upsetting to the balance of factors in the larger system of the plant.[8]

Measurement and values are part of the same system, each being both cause and effect of the other. Together they cast the present and forecast the future. When California schools classified Chicano children as retarded for testing low in English, the test measurements were being used to comply with social values and expectations. Conventional measurements create what conventional values demand—winners and losers, successes and failures. If we perceive the creation of losers and failures as counterproductive, we must find measurements to express and implement our perceptions and values. Conventional measurements express and implement the conventional values and expectations of hierarchies of authority.

Rank Has Its Privileges (RHIP)

There is a plethora of social commentary today but almost no good social measurement. Commentary is apart from the action, and too often it comprises a sardonic call to pessimism, despair, and dropping out. Measurement is active manipulating and controlling, a means of implementing values and objectives. Behind conventional commentaries like Rank Has Its Privileges (Perquisites or Payoffs), there lurks a conventional measurement. Pareto's law is behind RHIP.

The mathematical equation that Pareto devised apparently measures many socioeconomic phenomena. In graph form it appears as a negative exponential curve. Figure 3-1 shows how it expresses the distribution of income in the United States. As a rule of thumb sometimes used in business, it has been stated that 20 percent of the sales force makes 80 percent of the sales, and 20 percent of the effort produces 80 percent of the results. Conversely, the remaining 80 percent of the sales force produces only 20 percent of the sales, and the remaining 80 percent of the effort produces only 20 percent of the results.

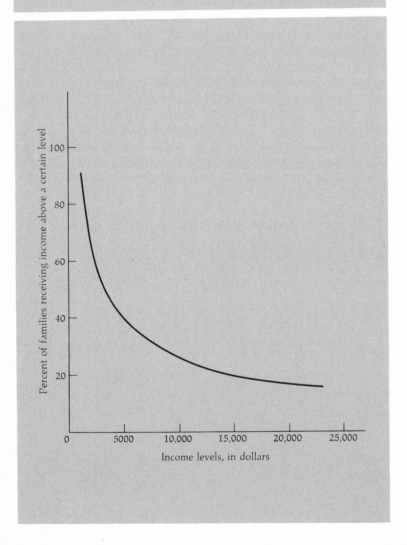

FIGURE 3-1
Distribution of Income in the United States
Pareto's negative exponential curve.

Pareto's law is empirical, not natural or intrinsic. In words, it is derived from the system, not imposed on it Pareto's law cuts both ways. If 20 percent of the effort produces 80 percent of the results, it is equally true that 20 percent of the jobs in a hierarchy provide 80 percent of the opportunities. If the remaining 80 percent of the effort produces only 20 percent of the results, it is equally true that 80 percent of the jobs in a hierarchy provide only 20 percent of the opportunities. Thus 80 percent of the jobs waste 80 percent of the human potentials of the conformed parts that fit the slots.

According to Goodwin Watson, "Our skill in exploiting the immense potentialities of the power of human cooperation has advanced very little from prehistoric times until rather recently."[9]

According to the American Assembly, Columbia University, in *The Changing World of Work in 1973*, "The individual worker and the society (at large) are changing much faster than institutions and the quality of the jobs they provide." The Assembly concludes: "Improving the place, the organization, and the nature of work can lead to better work performance and a better quality of life in the society. A crisis, though it may not presently exist, could confront us."[10]

PRODUCTIVITY OF SERVICE ORGANIZATIONS: THE PRODUCT OF FOUR OPERATING FUNCTIONS

The productivity of service organizations can be calculated as the product of four operating functions: (1) input, (2) processing, (3) output or follow-up, and (4) timing and coordination. If each function has a gross rating of 70 percent, the productivity of the organization in serving people is 24 percent gross. This is calculated simply as $.70 \times .70 \times .70 \times .70$.

For example, assume that 30 percent of those admitted to a state mental hospital do not require hospitalization but could be better treated as outpatients. Function one, input, would then have a gross rating of 70 percent. Assume that overcrowding and understaffing delay psychiatric attention, restrict therapy, and limit counseling. Lack of skills, understanding, or caring further reduce effective treatment. Function two, processing, might then have a rating lower than 10 or 20 percent (see the documentary movie

Titicutt Follies), but let us assume here that the rating is 50 percent. At this point, only seventy out of one hundred patients should be there and only half of the seventy are being helped. In other words, through function two, thirty-five patients are being helped and we have a productivity measurement of 35 percent gross. This is calculated by multiplying the ratings of the two functions: $.70 \times .50$.

Now assume that after discharge, outpatient services are limited and the patients must fend for themselves in the same environment where they were unable to cope before being committed. In fact, loss of job, setback in school, and family alienation may make the circumstances worse than before. Assume then that function three, output or follow-up, has a rating of 20 percent, meaning that one patient in five is being offered appropriate follow-up assistance. In other words, of the thirty-five patients who had been helped to the point of hospital discharge, only seven are given adequate follow-up. Organizational productivity is then calculated as 20 percent of 35 percent or 7 percent gross. Through function three, the calculation is $.70 \times .50 \times .20$.

Finally, we come to the fourth function, timing and coordination. The saying goes that there is a time and place for everything; economists refer to time-and-place utility. Too little too late is clearly as wasteful as too much too soon. For our example, recognize that the time of commitment of mental patients is often determined by the frustration point of relatives or police rather than the needs of the patient. The timing of both treatment and release is determined by availability of staff and their appraisal of priorities. Effective follow-up after discharge involves advance planning and preparation as well as communication and coordination with other institutions and agencies. Assume generously that the timing and coordination function can be given a 50 percent rating. The gross productivity of the organization in serving people is then finally calculated as half of 7 percent or $3\frac{1}{2}$ percent gross. In other words, out of one hundred patients admitted, three and one-half are effectively helped. This is calculated as $.70 \times .50 \times .20 \times .50$.

Gross productivity must be reduced to net productivity. If only $3\frac{1}{2}$ percent are effectively helped, what of the other $96\frac{1}{2}$ percent? If we assume, at a minimum, that injury is done to those who should not have been admitted, then injury to thirty people must be offset against the gain to three and one-half. Net productivity, assuming injury as great as gain, is a negative 26½ percent.

Measuring All Functions

The arithmetic is simple when it is accepted that there are indeed four related operating functions which must be appraised to determine organizational productivity. As we have seen, conventional measurements tend to constrict our view to one function only; for example, cost per inpatient in a mental hospital constricts our view to the processing function and ignores the input function (who is processed), the output or follow-up function (what happens to them), and the timing and coordination function (when processing and other functions take place). To view organizations in terms of one function only is to deny them goals or objectives. Without objectives there can be no accomplishment except by accident. When we apply conventional productivity measurements to single functions of service organizations we say, in effect, "It doesn't matter what you accomplish as long as you do whatever you are doing efficiently and at minimum cost."

To apply the conventional measurement of cost per inpatient to a mental hospital is to invite it to become a custodial warehouse, because the easiest way to reduce costs is to reduce treatments. Patient needs then become viewed as nuisances, as obstacles to achieving minimum costs. If we wish organizations to serve us instead of submerge us, we must require them to define their objectives for our review and approval. Then we must hold them responsible for achieving, in terms of all four operating functions, their approved service objectives.

A chain is no stronger than its weakest link. Similarly, the productivity of an organization can be no higher than the productivity of its weakest function. If any one of the four operating functions has a zero rating, the productivity of the organization, in terms of service to people, will be zero.

The Input Function. According to a recent federal survey, most crimes are unreported. According to a report on crime and punishment in America:

> While it can be assumed that most homicides or armed robberies get reported to the police, for many other statistically important crimes the reverse is true. This phenomenon is especially pronounced in violations by businessmen or middleclass criminals, or where criminal investigation would subject the victim to more emotional trauma (most sex cases), or where the attitude exists that calling the police won't do any good (burglary). No increase in police efficiency is going to have any effect in solving crimes that never become known to the police in the first place.[11]

What is proper input for a jail? First, we must decide on the objectives of incarceration pending trial or plea bargaining. Is it the deterrent effect on others? Punishment? Protection of society from imminent danger? Whatever the objective, the principal criterion in practice is poverty demonstrated by the inability to make bail. Rate the input function for jails less than 50 percent gross.

What of the input function for hospitals? As many as one-third of hospital admissions for surgery have been said to be for unnecessary operations. Some medical insurance encourages unnecessary admissions by covering diagnostic tests for patients in the hospital but not for outpatients. On the other hand, many who need hospital services do not seek them; recognizing this, some hospitals have established outreach clinics. Massachusetts General Hospital once voted not to undertake heart transplants until all children in the surrounding Roxbury ghetto were receiving routine immunization.

The Processing Function. In New York City over 90 percent of all criminal cases are settled by plea bargaining instead of trial. The bargaining is conducted on behalf of a defendant by a legal aid lawyer who spends only a few moments with the person he or she "defends." The overwhelming pressure is to plead guilty even if innocent. Courts administer their case loads, with the result that their productivity in terms of administering justice is close to zero.

Administering medications in a hospital is a vital process. Harmful side effects may offset possible benefits. We can infer that errors of omission or commission in giving medications occur as often as 10 percent of the time. This is difficult to measure or prove, especially from the outside, but it can be supported. If 10 percent error actually occurs, then anyone who has been hospitalized several days probably would have suffered an incident of incorrect or omitted medication. In response to my inquiries over a period of several years, more than twenty people told me of incidents involving them or their families and only one said he was unaware of any error. In regard to medication, many hospitals must be given a failing grade for this processing function (Figure 3-2).

Our schools are more and more devoted to testing, grading, and placing students, to judging and "measuring" their intellectual potential, and even to predicting their tendencies toward delinquency. Good teaching is then said to be that which results in achievement in line with potential. In other words, good teaching confirms the prophesies and makes them self-fulfilling. To the extent that tests of intellect, personality, and delinquent tendencies are inadequate and inappropriate, so then is processing in schools inadequate and inappropriate. If the simplistic organizations we create—like schools, hospitals, and other establishment hierarchies—fail in stating their objectives and measuring their own performance, it is logical to assume they fail in the infinitely more complex and inappropriate tasks of measuring the potential worth of human children and their development.

The Output or Follow-up Function. Output is often a complex process, not a simple act. The output of a symphony orchestra may be a concert or a recording, and either one requires skills in planning, staging, financing, and marketing. A concert which no one attends or a poor-quality recording which no one buys obviously vitiate any successful efforts in terms of the input and processing functions.

Sometimes output appears to be a single administrative act, such as sale of a product, discharge from a hospital, release from prison, or graduation from a school. But there is increasing recognition that follow-up processes are necessarily involved for achievement of organizational objectives. Product guarantees are given by businesses to follow up on sales. Halfway houses and social workers are now part of some follow-up processes for released mental patients. Parole supervision, however ineffective,

FIGURE 3-2
Administration of Drugs

Measurement of the processing function in the administration of drugs shows that many hospitals and nursing homes receive a failing grade.

IN HOSPITALS

For the thirty million patients hospitalized annually, the risk of adverse drug reactions is especially great. They are relatively older than non-hospitalized patients, they are usually more seriously ill, and they are exposed to more drugs during their hospital stay. It has been estimated that of the patients admitted to the medical services of general hospitals in the United States, each will receive an average of eight or more drugs during their hospitalization. As many as 28 percent of them may suffer an adverse reaction. Perhaps 3 to 5 percent of the patients in those medical services were admitted because of adverse reactions.

If admitted to the hospital for any other reason—a heart attack, a fractured leg, childbirth, or even a diagnostic procedure—a patient runs a substantial risk. In one early epidemiological study conducted in 1960, Dr. Elihu Schimmel of Yale found that of more than a thousand patients admitted during an eight-month period, 13 percent developed adverse drug reactions caused by diagnostic procedures or therapy. At least 1 percent of all admitted patients in this study died of an apparent drug reaction. Complicating the situation for hospitalized patients is the fact that from 2 to 8 percent of all drug doses given in hospitals are in error—wrong drug, wrong dose, wrong route of administration, wrong patient, or failure to give the prescribed drug.

Source: Milton Silverman and Philip R. Lee, *Pills, Profits, and Politics,* University of California Press, Berkeley, 1974.

IN NURSING HOMES

A report by a Senate subcommittee on the use of drugs in the nation's 23,000 nursing homes, released today, concluded that many elderly patients "may often actually suffer setbacks in physical well-being because of poor management, or worse, of prescription drugs given to them."

The systems for distributing or administering drugs to patients are generally "inefficient and ineffective," with the result that 20 to 40 percent "are administered in error," and there is a "high incidence" of adverse reactions.

The report stated that the "management of drugs in nursing homes often was the responsibility of untrained personnel," who were described by an aide, quoted in the report, as "seldom knowing the difference between 'an aspirin and a mothball.'"

Source: Linda Charlton, "Misuse of Drugs Reported in Nation's Nursing Homes," *The New York Times,* Jan. 17, 1975.

is a follow-up process, and most prisoners are released on parole. Medicare officially recognizes that nursing care may be part of a necessary follow-up process after hospital discharge.

Of course, hierarchical organizations try to lay any output measurements on people. Schools assign class rankings to their graduates instead of measuring their own output of educational services. The greater the number of students that schools reject or decline to serve, the higher they assert their standards and performance to be. For the purposes of functional measurement of productivity, however, students who flunk out, drop out, and are turned off must be reckoned as part of the output of educational institutions. So viewed, few educational institutions would get a passing grade for output.

Feedback is now understood to be an essential element in learning, developing, decision making, and controlling. To set up an organization without including an output or follow-up function is to deny it feedback. Without feedback an organization cannot learn, develop, improve in decision making, or effectively exercise self-control. In addition, we can induce from looking at cybernetic feedback, as in the thermostat-furnace loop, that a statement of objective, like desired temperature, must be plugged in. Thus we find that organizations without stated objectives are unable to use feedback. In other words, organizations lacking either output, follow-up functions, or stated objectives are deprived of feedback and, therefore, are unable to learn, develop, and improve.

The Timing and Coordination Function. When is a mental patient ready for discharge? At Bronx State Mental Hospital the patients were given the freedom to walk out when they felt ready, which, of course, made them responsible for themselves. In hierarchies of authority, only lip service can be given to freedom because freedom and responsibility go hand in hand. In hierarchies, decisions by authorities supplant and suppress individual judgment and responsibility for questions of timing. Schools, for example, decide how long it should take to learn prescribed material. Obviously their time allowance is suitable only for an average student and painful for students toward either end of a normal distribution. If we accept one standard deviation plus or minus from the midpoint of the distribution as not significantly disturbing, then 68 percent of all students will fit the pattern and 32 percent will not. With 32 percent of its students out of phase, a school must be considered failing in its timing function.

No educational objective for prescribing standard learning periods seems to exist. The apparent purposes are administrative convenience and sustaining the authority of the hierarchy. And the responses to failure fit the basic hierarchical process. Test, label, and blame the victims, and segregate them in slower or faster classes. Conventional measurements serve the hierarchy in controlling and manipulating people. If people want schools to serve them, the schools must state their objectives and the schools must be measured.

As to coordination, William Glasser[12] describes how all employees in a mental institution, including gardeners and cleaning help, were trained to be part of the team in treating patients. Coordination was built around shared objectives and the responsibility of each employee in achieving the objectives. An organization chart under his plan would show the patient in the middle with lines radiating out to each employee. In contrast, a hierarchy achieves coordination by establishing lines of authority and standard procedures. Objectives are unstated and responsibility is denied except to follow orders. Naturally a hierarchy will find measurements and make self-fulfilling prophesies to show that no higher level of coordination can be achieved. In fact, however, the hierarchical organization must be graded a failure in coordination because it can achieve only mechanical, perfunctory, subhuman coordination. This achievement may be valuable in manufacturing, but it is not worth much in rendering services like health care, education, or justice.

Summarizing the Measurements

If each of its four functions rates as 60 percent, the productivity of an organization is 13 percent gross. This is calculated as $.60 \times .60 \times .60 \times .60$. If each of its four functions rates as 50 percent, the productivity of an organization is 6 percent gross. If any function is missing, gross productivity is zero. Shocking as it may seem, low results are typical. Gross productivity under 20 percent gross appears to be the rule rather than the exception.

From gross productivity we must subtract the damage that organizations inflict, such as unnecessary surgical operations, unjust punishments, and creation of failures. This damage is obviously substantial, and we must face up to the stunning fact that net productivity for many or most Established Model service organizations is close to zero or is negative. In the next chapter, we will try to describe what this means in terms of people. In later chapters, we will try to describe what this means in terms of the methods of organizational improvement and of personal defense.

CONCLUSION

There is a linkage between how we look at the world and how we act. That linkage is measurement, and it expresses our set and setting. When we select a measurement or one is applied to us, it controls goals, motivation, and behavior. Thus, measurement should be used as a tool and not viewed as the revelation of some kind of impartial or objective truth. This chapter has described the conventional patterns of measurement, which show the productivity of people in serving organizations, and new patterns of measurement, which show the productivity of service organizations in serving people. When we measure organizations, we control them. When organizations measure us, they control us.

NOTES

[1] *City-Wide Productivity Program Report,* Aug. 7, 1972.

[2] *Measuring and Enhancing Productivity in the Federal Sector,* U.S. Government Printing Office, Washington, D.C., Aug. 4, 1972.

[3] *53rd Annual Report,* National Bureau of Economic Research, Inc., New York, September 1973.

[4] Robinson's law is a paraphrase of one of Parkinson's laws, as expressed by Daniel Robinson, a partner of Peat, Marwick, Mitchell & Co., who has worked extensively with nonprofit organizations.

[5] J. George Harrar, *Strategy toward the Conquest of Hunger,* The Rockefeller Foundation, New York, 1967.

[6] *Accounting Review,* the 1971 supplement to Volume XLVI, contained several articles on measurement theory and referred in several places to surrogate measurements.

[7] David Sirota, "Productivity Management," *Harvard Business Review,* vol. 44, p. 111, September 1966.

[8] Goodwin Watson, *Social Psychology,* J. B. Lippincott Company, Philadelphia, 1968, pp. 543–544.

[9] Ibid., p. 109.

[10] The American Assembly, Columbia University, *The Changing World of Work in 1973,* Report of the Forty-third American Assembly, Nov. 1–4, 1973, Arden House, Harriman, N.Y., pp. 4, 10.

[11] American Friends Service Committee, *Struggle for Justice: A Report on Crime and Punishment in America,* Hill & Wang, Inc., New York, 1971. Reprinted with permission of Farrar, Straus & Giroux, Inc.

[12] William Glasser, *Reality Therapy,* Harper & Row, Publishers, Incorporated, New York, 1965, pp. 109, 111.

FOUR

Taking the Triple Whammy from Established Model Organizations

There is only one apex in a hierarchical pyramid regardless of its size. Thus there is only one president in a dairy cooperative whether it has 100 members or 100,000. But the bigger a hierarchy, the more subordinates and inferiors within its ranks.

Large continuing organizations appeared mostly in this century. In 1910 my father taught in a one-room schoolhouse which had twelve students; some sixty years later I lectured at City University of New York which had over two hundred thousand. During the same period, civilian employment in the federal government increased sevenfold to almost three million. In 1910 the societal model provided for independent workers who were neither superiors nor inferiors, while today the societal model calls for homogenized, conformed parts in large, homogenized, organizational settings. Nowadays, it is said, "If you've seen one, you've seen them all."

Along with this century's growth in the size of organizations, there has been a peculiar subversion of the organizational role which was once stated to be "of, by, and for the people." Even farmer cooperatives, as they have grown, have turned against the farmers who created them. And there has been a fearsome growth in the processes by which organizations extend and amplify their authority over the individuals they subsume.

PROCESSES OF THE TRIPLE WHAMMY

Winners are displayed as symbols of the system and its rewards— the winning home-run hitter and the crowd cheering, the winning politician and his limousine, the movie star receiving her award in expensive gown and jewels. But symbols don't help us understand ourselves and what is being done to us. Nor do they help us understand the workings of the system. Before going on to look at ourselves instead of at symbols, however, we shall take a brief look at hierarchical processes. They fall into three categories: (1) ranking—assigning us to our places, (2) enforcing—keeping us in our places, and (3) rejecting—excluding us or casting us out.

Ranking

On May 27, 1974, while baptizing my grandson Trent, my friend Dermi addressed himself to the baby: "The purpose of this cere- mony, Trent, is to symbolize your acceptance into this family. You are accepted not for your future successes or because you will be without fault or sin. You are accepted and loved for yourself."

Established Model Organizations interview you, test you, com- pare you with others, evaluate your potentials and tendencies, grade, sort, and label you, weigh the power and influence of your family and friends along with your other credentials, decide your place, and finally either reject you or accept you probationally. All, of course, in accordance with the charitable, educational, or other humanitarian purposes for which the organizations were estab- lished.

The old charity, some say, is obsolete. To feed the starving may be wrong because then they can survive and propagate. With an increased population in the world there can only be more starvation in the next generation and risk of permanent damage to the entire ecosystem.

Only his family accepts Trent.

Enforcing

To keep you in your place, Established Organizations must stop you from learning, and they do this by denying you purpose or objectives, demanding compliance with prescribed methods and procedures, rewarding repetition and punishing mistakes. To increase efficiency, organizations strive to simplify your tasks so you can work at ever lower and more routine levels until you can be replaced by a computer or machine. The management term for this process is *work simplification;* the human term is *downgrading* or *degradation.*

To overcome your initial resistance, organizations indoctrinate and socialize you. Total institutions like prisons, navy ships, and hospitals mortify and strip you (Figure 4-1). To ensure that you conform, organizations police you, check up on you, and audit you and establish elaborate systems of internal control. These are the methods of management and administration.

Psychologists pick up where teachers and administrators leave off. Using techniques of behavior modification, such as aversion therapy and operant conditioning, they program people to be less trouble to organizations. With all kindness and goodwill, they find values beyond freedom and dignity in molding subordinates to fit those patterns and systems decided upon by hierarchical superiors. Psychologists, like psychiatrists, are trained to work on people and to help them adapt to the system—the vast expansion in the need for such help can be interpreted as an indictment of organizational behavior and the need for its modification.

Rejecting

Is it true or false that for every winner there has to be a loser? False—there has to be a continuing supply of losers if a winner is to keep on winning. In schools, grading on a curve theoretically means that the A student needs an F student at the other end of the normal distribution; then annually or more often, when the F student is eliminated or drops out, another student must be pushed into the failing position. In sports, the winner needs a waiting list of losers who will challenge, fail, and drop out. In government, decision makers at the top of the hierarchy order actions to produce unemployed workers in their attempt to conquer inflation. And some economists observe that profit-making companies seem to survive only by establishing a large pool of marginal workers who can be picked up when needed and dropped when business is slow.

Of course, brief descriptions oversimplify, and when we view school grading in small segments, it may not seem to involve rejection. Schools in exclusive suburbs do not produce so many failures and neither do graduate schools in universities. Instead they assume their students are mostly in the upper half of a normal

FIGURE 4-1
Authority in Total Institutions

The processes of authority show starkly in total institutions such as boarding schools, camps, hospitals, prisons, and nursing homes.

The *stripping processes* through which *mortification of the self* occurs are fairly standard in our total institutions. Personal identity equipment is removed, as well as other possessions with which the inmate may have identified himself, there typically being a system of nonaccessible storage from which the inmate can only reobtain his effects should he leave the institution. As a substitute for what has been taken away, institutional issue is provided, but this will be the same for large categories of inmates and will be regularly repossessed by the institution. In brief, standardized defacement will occur. . . . Family, occupational, and educational career lines are chopped off, and a stigmatized status is submitted. Sources of fantasy materials which had meant momentary releases from stress in the home world are denied. Areas of autonomous decision are eliminated through the process of collective scheduling of daily activity. Many channels of communication with the outside are restricted or closed off completely. Verbal discreditings occur in many forms as a matter of course. Expressive signs of respect for the staff are coercively and continuously demanded. And the effect of each of these conditions is multiplied by having to witness the mortification of one's fellow inmates. . . .

In the background of the sociological stripping process, we find a characteristic authority system with three distinctive elements, each basic to total institutions.

First, to a degree, authority is of the *echelon* kind. Any member of the staff class has certain rights to discipline any member of the inmate class. . . . In our society, the adult himself, however, is typically under the authority of a *single* immediate superior in connection with domestic duties. The only echelon authority he must face—the police—typically are neither constantly nor relevantly present, except perhaps in the case of traffic-law enforcement.

Second, the authority of corrective sanctions is directed to a great multitude of items of conduct of the kind that are constantly occurring and constantly coming up for judgment; in brief, authority is directed to matters of dress, deportment, social intercourse, manners and the like. . . .

The third feature of authority in total institutions is that misbehaviors in one sphere of life are held against one's standing in other spheres. Thus, an individual who fails to participate with proper enthusiasm in sports may be brought to the attention of the person who determines where he will sleep and what kind of work task will be accorded to him.

When we combine these three aspects of authority in total institutions, we see that the inmate cannot easily escape from the press of judgmental officials and from the enveloping tissue of constraint. The system of authority undermines the basis for control that adults in our society expect to exert over their interpersonal environment and may produce the terror of feeling that one is being radically demoted in the age-grading system.

Source: Erving Goffman, "Characteristics of Total Institutions," as quoted in *Deviance,* edited by Simon Dinitz, et al., Oxford University Press, New York, 1969.

distribution. Conversely, however, there are schools which assume their students are mostly in the lower half of a normal distribution. In one vocational high school in New York, no teacher could give a grade above C without special approval by the principal. In a ghetto high school a department head told me that only one student in a specified class of twenty was capable of learning. I knew the students were capable and interested, but sure enough, nineteen dropped out and failed. Overall, grading in schools is a process that produces failures and accomplishes rejecting.

Winners are custom-made, but losers are mass-produced. Processes of mass rejection include prejudice, discrimination, and dealing with measurements instead of people. Processes of denial and concealment not only create losers but make them invisible. The poor are segregated in urban slums and rural backwoods. Prisons and mental institutions are located in isolated areas. And the legal system systematically supports these processes of mass rejection by denying full human status to children, women, inmates of total institutions, and ex-convicts as well as to those who are poor or lacking in institutional credentials.

ARE YOU AN OBJECT OF THE TRIPLE WHAMMY?

Organizational processes can be evaluated in terms of nonproductive responses to them. The responses include allergies, asthma, hypertension, or ulcers; alcohol, amphetamines, barbiturates, heroin, overeating; apathy, despair, fear, self-pity, or violence; apple polishing, compliance, gratitude, self-deprecation, and scripting. How do you react and who are you? Asking who you are, of course, is asking a rhetorical question. The real question is how you are classified, and we shall proceed to that question.

Are You Old?

Ten percent of the United States population is over sixty-five years of age. In most organizations this is the compulsory retirement age, because on the average you are no longer considered useful after sixty-five. If you persist in finding work after retirement, you will be penalized by reduction of your Social Security benefits. In other words, not only do organizations treat you on the average, but they also insist that you act that way instead of as a unique human being.

Compulsory retirement is an attempt to solve organizational problems, not to get work done. It is a process of rejection which is commonly followed by segregating you in a retirement community, golden-age apartment, nursing home, or rooming house. Pathetically, you may perceive enforced idleness as more meaningful and pleasant than the "productive years" which preceded it.

> "Senility" is an invention of modern Western society. It is one of the most damaging, self-fulfilling prophecies ever devised. So thoroughly have we been brainwashed by this false concept that we fail to recognize how destructive our thoughts and actions can be. . . . Yet there is growing evidence that so-called senility is much more a functional withdrawal from painful experiences than it is the end result of physical deterioration. A main cause of senility is social. Forced to retire on substandard income, robbed of his identity, devoid of purpose, his spirit crushed, the older person turns away and adjusts as best he can to a hostile environment.
>
> We behave according to reality as we perceive it. Many "symptoms of senility" are normal behavior when considered in context with the person's life situation. [1]

Jules Henry observed and defined the reciprocating processes of distortion and withdrawal. [2] They are illustrated here by a fictionalized incident at a home for old men. [3]

> In a barrackslike room the beds are lined up close together with just enough space for a straight chair between the beds. Most of the men are sitting in chairs doing nothing, a few are in bed, and a few are down the hall in a television room.
>
> As an aide walks by with an armful of fresh linen, one of the old men calls softly but tensely, "I've got to get to the toilet." Apparently the aide does not hear. He starts repeating the sentence to no one in particular until an orderly passes with bottles of specimens; then the sentence is louder but apparently the orderly does not hear. The repetition becomes louder as the aide passes in the opposite direction with an armful of soiled linen, "Later Pop, I'm busy."

> The old man stands up, moves a few faltering steps, falls, urinates and defecates. There is a commotion and he is picked up and laid on his bed until the orderly gets a chance to clean him. "What a mess," someone says.
>
> Twenty-four hours later the old man calls again, the same sentence, but the voice is louder and edged with panic. The aide passes, then the orderly, and their faces show exasperation, "Not so loud, Pop. You're disturbing people."
>
> The old man lies down on the bed, urinates and defecates. When the orderly gets around to cleaning him, he says, "If you can't take care of yourself, you can't stay here." Two days later the old man is transferred to the ward for those who are incontinent, disruptive, or bedridden. He stays in bed.

In response to each sign of weakness, each deviation from normal, society took a step away from the old man. Step by step as society rejected him and withdrew from him, the old man's behavior became further distorted.

Are You a Student?

Twenty-nine percent of the United States population is in school; three-and-a-half percent is in college or graduate school. In most schools the primary goals are to transmit culture: to socialize you and prepare you to take your place as a conformed or excluded part in the outside world. To achieve their primary goals, schools give primary attention to the hierarchical processes of ranking and enforcing, denying and rejecting you.

The purpose of education is your achievement of optimal growth and development as an individual, an achievement which most schools can tolerate in only small doses if at all because it subverts their primary goals. Accordingly, many of the processes of education are ignored or taboo in schools, like observation and induction, problem recognition, boundary changing, trial and error, self-motivation, goal setting, priority setting, acceptance of feedback, and dissent.

Like senility, adolescence is an imposed social condition, not a natural one. Peter Drucker[4] defines it as the status of adults, ages fifteen through twenty-five or more, who are students and therefore are treated as children and required to act like them. As a child, decisions must be made for you because you cannot decide wisely for yourself, and you must be rewarded and punished. With up to ten years or even more of adulthood-childhood as preparation, you are well prepared for the parent-child transactions of the hierarchies in which you will continue your life.

Yesterday we recognized that education opened the door to opportunity. Today we must recognize that when the door to opportunity is locked, it precludes effective education. In the United States today, about one-third of the population is "poor or at risk," excluded by the system or hanging in by their fingernails (Figure 4-2). They are the losers, failures, marginal workers, and unemployed who enable those within the system to be winners, conformed parts, and more or less secure and regular workers. Schools initiate the rejection and exclusion processes, and they have devised special strategies for generating the necessary frustration, futility, and failure on the part of both students and teachers. These stratagems have been well documented in recent books, such as *Death at an Early Age*,[5] *Walk the White Line*,[6] and *How Children Fail*,[7] but they are new only in the documentation of their massive application.

"Knowing is a process not a product," according to Bruner[8] and others. If you are a student, have they in your school taught you the process?

Are You a Worker?

Thirty-eight percent of the United States population is gainfully employed. If you are a worker, you are at the bottom of the hierarchy like your predecessors who were serfs, slaves, indentured servants, bonded laborers, and children. The social revolutions which freed the slaves and removed children from the work force did not improve your position, because every human advance impacting on organizations has inspired new techniques for control. In the early part of the twentieth century, the new techniques were developed under the name of *scientific management* or *Taylorism*. Today computers are used and new Orwellian controls have names like *data banks, information systems,* and *decision theory*.

In the annual report of the Graduate School of Business of Columbia University for 1969–1970, Dean George James projected the scene as follows[9]: "In these developments [information systems

FIGURE 4-2

The Excluded One-Third

A measure of those outside the system.

In each of the recent years, the Census Bureau has estimated that there are about 25 million unrelated individuals or people in families with incomes below the poverty level. . . . On the other hand, over 50 million Americans, or about a quarter of the total population, were below the poverty level in at least one of these [six] years. . . . In fact, the Panel data suggest as many as 85 million persons, 40 percent of the total population, were eligible for welfare [Public Assistance, Food Stamps or Public Housing] benefits at some point during the six years of the Panel.

Poor and at risk [families are defined as] those 35 percent of all families which fell into one of the two lowest deciles of the family income/needs distribution [the lowest quintile] *at least once* over the five years.

*   *   *

In the analysis of involuntary work losses due to unemployment we find the expected result that unemployment is more serious among workers with low wage jobs. There are also strong independent effects of education and occupation. The education effect is particularly striking. High school dropouts experience unemployment levels approximately double those of high school graduates. The reduction in risk of unemployment resulting from completion of high school is not as great for non-whites as for whites.

*   *   *

When we consider non-contributory transfers, or welfare, we find that virtually all families with no other income receive welfare, and their benefits average to about 75% of what the family needs to feed, house, and clothe itself. There is, however, a large inequity for families with some very low income from other sources: a large fraction of these families receive no welfare at all, and on the average, they have a total income equal to just half of their need standard.

Source: U.S. Dept. of Health, Education, and Welfare, *The Changing Economic Status of 5000 American Families: Highlights from the Panel Study of Income Dynamics*, conducted by the University of Michigan Institute for Social Research, May 1974.

and decision theory] there is the possibility of a major swing back toward corporate centralization in which most decisions of moment might be made by a handful of senior general executives in the head office." The report continues with a discussion of the elite education and experience necessary to develop the "very wise and experienced senior executives," "the wise men at the top."

The book *Effective Managerial Leadership* by James J. Cribbin, [10] says:

> Whether the advocates of permissiveness like it or not, no society can long endure without authority. As Thomas Aquinas averred, even in a society of saints in heaven, there will be a need for order, and order stems primarily from authority.
>
> Authority, in its simplest definition, is a right to obligate subordinates to carry out assigned tasks, execute legitimate directives, and generally perform as required in justice. No organization has lasted without acting upon the need to assign the few the right to determine objectives, make crucial decisions, define relevant behavior, and reward and punish according to the demands of those who have been entrusted with the welfare of that organization.

In other words, management theory is aimed primarily at maintaining and enhancing the hierarchy of authority and keeping you, the worker, in your place. But for all its controls, management theory is incredibly ineffective in getting work done. Cribbin states that "estimates of the index of efficiency at which people work in industry range from 10 to 25 percent."[11] Such estimates happily confirm managements' assumption that you are incompetent, stupid, and shiftless. Just as teachers cannot function without students, or parents without children, management cannot function and be rewarded as decision makers and bosses unless you fill the role of unthinking and reluctant worker.

From assumption, prophecy, and system-serving measurements, organizations derive the rationale to treat you as the enemy and hit you with the triple whammy. As a worker, you are ranked, conditioned, rejected, and displaced by organizations, in relentless sequence.

Are You a Member of a
Minority Race or Religion?

Over 12 percent of the United States population is nonwhite. Add Puerto Ricans, who are classified as white but treated otherwise. Include Indians and Chicanos. Add Jews and members of other minority religions. Add those with long hair or odd "foreign" names. All in all, at least 20 percent of the United States population is some kind of visible minority.[12] If you are a member of a minority, you know there are restrictions on where and how you live, study, work, and play.

Why are there ghettos, barrios, Chinatowns, reservations, communes, shantytowns, and restricted suburbs? Why are minorities put in special low-level, dead-end entry jobs? Why are minorities the last hired and first fired? Why have minorities been the targets of organized social violence? Is prejudice an intrinsic flaw in human nature or is the system to blame? If you are a member of a minority, these are not academic questions.

Whatever the origins of segregation and discrimination, and whatever human needs or weaknesses they serve, one thing is clear—the hierarchy needs and exploits them. In terms of its conventional measurements of efficiency, how better could the system fill the bottom rows in the hierarchical pyramid and keep them filled? In terms of its conventional measurements, how better could the system mass-produce the losers which it needs? In terms of its conventional measurements, how better could the system deny and reject the growing percentage of the population which it must exclude?

If you are a member of a minority, do you understand why the system blames its victims and asserts their inherent inferiority? Or has understanding been at the wrong level in your hierarchy of needs?

Are You a Female?

A little over 50 percent of the population of the United States is female. If you are a female, male voices have revealed to you a male god who created you to comfort man and assuage his loneliness. By law and by custom you are deterred from developing an independent identity. Symbolically you abandon your name when you marry. Your success is still commonly defined as influence rather than accomplishment. Both Fascist dictators and Republican presidents have defined your place as in the home taking care of your children.

Given the right to vote, you are still denied your ability to think. By nature females are supposed to be emotional instead of logical, as if centering on objectives, which is what emotions do, is not an essential part of thinking. Indulgently you acknowledge that men are pompous asses, but it ill behooves you to be indulgent.

As a woman, you started being liberated by converting the affective into the cognitive and by developing a self-image that was independent of the way institutions wanted you to be for their convenience. But the reality of your gains is less than the appearance.

Are You a Winner?

Maslow[13] found patterns of behavior that characterize losers. These patterns have been displayed by Arabian women of the era when they were considered to be property rather than people, by slaves on plantations, by children of highly authoritative parents, by workers, and from Maslow's own experiments and observations, by monkeys low in the pecking order. Are there corresponding patterns of behavior that characterize winners? Have these patterns been displayed by chauvinistic men, slave owners, highly authoritative parents, supervisors, bosses, and monkeys high in the pecking order? The answer, of course, must be "yes." Winners as well as losers are stereotypes.

Winners require status symbols such as the black belt of a karate expert or a reserved place in the parking lot. They require deference, agreement, praise, and applause. The perfect stereotype of a big winner in politics or entertainment is found in the responses to media which are not sufficiently deferential: "biased," "picking on me," and "anyway, all female reporters are hookers." Bluster and pomposity are sad to see, but the perversion of economic and governmental institutions to support a stereotype is a total disaster.

Winners as stereotypes symbolize the system, support the status quo, and proclaim the need for law, order, and privilege. They are defensive, and their arrogance is a defense mechanism. They subordinate morality and personal integrity to the system. When they feel helpless, they resort to incredible acts of verbal and physical violence.

Winners, like losers, are engulfed and overwhelmed by the system, and it seems that they seek psychiatric help at least as often as losers do. Berne[14] asserts that losers resist when a psychiatrist attempts to make them into winners, preferring instead to become brave losers. In other words, losers desire help in coping, in becoming meaningful individuals instead of conformed parts. Whoever you are and however you are classified—winner, loser, old, student, worker, minority, female—perhaps your greatest need is to learn a methodology for withstanding the onslaught of the system, for countering the dehumanizing processes of the triple whammy.

CONCLUSION

Assuming your characteristics to be innate, the system ranks, conditions, rejects, and forces your reaction to its appraisal of your worth. Only by learning to react effectively to the processes of hierarchical organizations can you be your own person, living your own life, achieving your own skills, accomplishing your own goals. Criticism and resentment are ineffective reactions. Chapters 5 through 9 present effective ones.

NOTES

[1] *What Are You? I Am Old,* New York State Communities Aid Association, 1972.

[2] Jules Henry, *Culture against Man,* Random House, Inc., New York, 1963.

[3] This fictionalized incident was synthesized from the nature of work experiences in nursing homes reported by my wife Olga Heaton, a registered nurse, and my daughter Frances Brancato, who has empathy for older people.

[4] Peter Drucker, *Age of Discontinuity,* Harper & Row, Publishers, Incorporated, New York, 1969.

[5] Jonathan Kozol, *Death at an Early Age,* Bantam Books, Inc., New York, 1970.

[6] Elizabeth M. Eddy, *Walk the White Line,* Frederick A. Praeger, Inc., New York, 1965.

[7] John Holt, *How Children Fail*, Pitman Publishing Corporation, New York, 1964.

[8] Jerome S. Bruner, quoted in Robert F. Biehler, *Psychology Applied to Teaching*, Houghton Mifflin Company, Boston, 1971, p. 185.

[9] Columbia University, The Graduate School of Business, *Report for the Year 1969-70*, New York, 1970, pp. 1-2.

[10] James J. Cribbin, *Effective Managerial Leadership*, American Management Association, New York, 1972, pp. 86-87.

[11] Ibid., p. 106.

[12] *The American Almanac*, Grosset & Dunlap, Inc., New York, 1973.

[13] Abraham Maslow, *Euspsychian Management*, Dow Jones–Irwin, Inc., Homewood, Ill., 1965.

[14] Eric Berne, *What Do You Say After You Say Hello?*, Grove Press, Inc., New York, 1972. Berne referred to losers resisting becoming winners in this book.

FIVE

Changing People Problems to Work Problems

At the level of Physical Force, the problem is to control people. At the level of Authority, the problems are to rank, police, and reject people. At the level of Influence, we try to exploit, condition, and indoctrinate people. At the Fusion level, people are accepted and we try to arrive at a consensus on goals and methods; at this level, the problems are work, working procedures, and coordination. At the Development level, the focus is still on work, with measurements of organizational performance and then feedback to produce changes in structure, work goals, and work methods.

"R. J. is just too stupid to work here," exploded the assistant supervisor of the payroll department. "Five months in a row, the same dumb mistake. Get me someone good or I can't be responsible." Back in the payroll department a clerk was trembling.

"Cut the histrionics," was my response, and I ran off a string of questions. "Tell me exactly what happened five months ago. Who found the mistake? How? How should it have been found? Who corrected it? Was R. J. told? What did R. J. say? Do you have written procedures? How have you changed your review procedures in the last five months? Not until we know that our instructions and procedures are as good as we can make them will we consider whether R. J. is good enough for the job. Now let's get down to business."

Most people are locked into the Established Perception Model. To release them and move them up the Hierarchy of Methods, I stumbled on an idea which I have repeated a hundred times: "In the Comptroller's Office our concern is work, not personalities." Living by these words is tough and productive, but it is also warmly human because the unspoken corollary is that people are accepted. Success is not a simple matter of attitude and intent, however. Instead it is a matter of applying the right processes with sufficient skill. The processes of working together will be introduced in this chapter.

ARRIVING AT A CONSENSUS

Alienation, dissent, and divergent views are sources of conflict and waste, but they can also be sources of innovation and productivity improvement. According to a survey, managers spend 20 percent of their time dealing with conflict situations. In a hierarchy of authority, the basic techniques are to prevent, gloss over, or suppress conflict, but these techniques also suppress innovation and productivity improvement. In the Target Organizational Model, conflict situations are not avoided; instead they are dealt with by the processes of arriving at a consensus, namely, communicating, confronting, factfinding, and negotiating. In a hierarchy of authority, these are the methods of crisis intervention. In the Target Model, at the Fusion level, these are basic continuous organizational processes for getting useful work done effectively, that is, for improving productivity.

Communicating

In the sense of interchanging thoughts and knowledge, there is no place for communicating in the Established Organizational Model. Listening is for subordinates, and speaking is for superiors. Mark the words of superiors because speaking with authority means speaking with knowledge. Conversely, speaking without credentials or authority means speaking from ignorance and no one need listen. Thus subordinates are to be seen and overseen, not heard. And teachers need listen only to correct.

Information systems are designed to supply superiors with what is needed to make decisions and give orders. Therefore, information systems process only data specified in advance, excluding anything about (1) objectives, which superiors are assumed to have within themselves, (2) methods, which superiors are supposed to prescribe down the chain of command, and (3) anything else unasked for or unwelcome. Superiors receive what they hope to receive, because that is what subordinates must give them to stay out of trouble. In the Established Model, superiors end up surrounded by people who automatically agree with them because that is the way the system works.

> Under pressure to show results, United States infantry in Vietnam scrounged up enemy paraphernalia to support fictitious reports of enemy casualties. Such reports were accumulated and fed into the Pentagon's information system. Year after year the data led to renewed decisions that we were winning and renewed predictions that victory was close at hand.

Throw explanations into a chain of command and subordinates say, "Just tell me what to do." Throw objectives or methods into an information system and managers say, "Just do what you are told and I will make the decisions." To start communicating, the first step is to change perception models and think in terms of feedback. The second step is to talk about work, not rank, about objectives and methods, not information systems and decision theory. The third step is to make a commitment to pay the costs and learn the values of having associates instead of superiors and inferiors.

Confronting

In the Established Organizational Model, higher-ups in the hierarchy perceive a confrontation as a breakdown in law and order, something threatening and hostile. As a concept, confrontation is merely a direct approach, open and honest (see Figure 5-1). In the Target Organizational Model, confrontation is one of the four essential processes in arriving at a consensus. In daily life it may

FIGURE 5-1

Confrontation

A process of arriving at a consensus.

Confrontation is a direct approach. It means that you say what you see, hear, or experience, directly, forthrightly, and clearly. There are no value judgments inherent in the concept of confrontation—no right or wrong, good or bad. It is a straightforward, direct means of communicating as opposed to covert, mystifying, or other indirect methods.

This direct approach is not necessarily a destructive assault or a perceived insult although it may be perceived as such by others who are attuned to indirect approaches to people and problems. Directness is viewed as hostile and aggressive in our society. Children are socialized not to say what they see, not to report what they hear, and not to communicate what they feel and experience. When they learn these "not's" very well, they are rewarded by being given adult status. The classic story of the Emperor's New Clothes gives us a rather beautiful illustration of the essential clarity, openness, directness, and honesty of children as opposed to adults who habitually use mystification, sham, and "as if."

Directness is not an expression of anger, meanness, or viciousness. Directness is a cool, cognitive, reasoned approach. Statements of feeling are made just as directly as statements of thought, opinion, or action, but angry feelings as an overtone need not permeate and overshadow the aims of the exchange. The aim of confrontation is to focus on an issue, not on the personalities or the personal faults of the interactors.

Source: Shirley A. Smoyak, Ph.D., "The Confrontation Process," *American Journal of Nursing,* September 1974, Vol. 74, No. 9.

seem difficult to confront or be confronted, but confrontation can be avoided only by being irresponsible. A doctor must tell the patient when an operation is needed.

When we avoid confrontation, it is because personalities, not work, control our behavior. When we live up to confrontation, it is because work, not personalities, controls our behavior. In the Target Model, confrontation is based on accepting people and including them. Avoiding confrontation is a way of rejecting and excluding.

> Twenty years ago when I was a supervisor in a public account-
> ing firm, a staff accountant confronted me. "On our first job
> together, Herb," he said, "you told me that criticism of my
> work was an investment of your time in teaching me. You said
> that as long as you criticized my work, I could know you
> believed in me and my future. So now on this last job you
> haven't said anything. Does that mean that my work is perfect
> or have you written me off?"

Where the organizational processes are ranking, enforcing, and rejecting, members of the organization perceive exposure of mis-takes as a personal danger. One night quite late an agitated senior officer phoned me and blurted out, "You have to cover for me." Coverup is the alternative to confrontation. If openness and straight talk about work are too great a risk, then pretense and deviousness are the safe alternatives. Of course, pretense and deviousness are not sources of improved productivity. Confronta-tion is, but it can flourish only where people are accepted and included.

Fact Finding

In the last of the ninth inning, score tied, bases loaded, full count on the batter—three and two—the pitcher throws, the batter takes, and the umpire hesitates. The batter whirls and cries, "What is it?" And the umpire retorts, "It's nothing until I call it." In a jury trial, the jurors determine the facts, meaning they decide whether to believe witnesses or to accept other evidence as ringing true. Thus facts are created by authority, viewpoint, perception models, and levels of awareness or consciousness (see Figure 5-2).

FIGURE 5-2
What We Perceive

It is different from the outside looking in.

The course was entitled "Making It on Your Own—Running a Business or Selling Your Services," and I taught it to a class of prisoners in a maximum security prison. My wife attended every class.

A certified public accountant from one of the big public accounting firms was guest lecturer on costs and tax deductions. A prisoner interrupted him, "What if the tax people come along and say you did wrong and put you in prison?"

"But you have evidence," replied the accountant.

"All evidence is political," said the prisoner.

"No, no," said the accountant, "I mean things like invoices and cancelled checks," and he went on from there.

*　　*　　*

During the next week I told this story several times because it moved me.

1. Businessman: "Of course. First I decide to fire someone, then I build the record to justify it."

2. Personnel person: "He's sick. To say evidence is political is just an excuse for what he did."

3. Former Vista volunteer: "Can you visualize his world and what he was talking about? For example . . ."

4. Luncheon group consisting of three Ph.D.'s—a social scientist, an historian, a physicist—and a former Army officer: "How stupid to say all evidence is political. His IQ must be pathetic."

*   *   *

Definition of Evidence—that which supports our opinions or conclusions.

Definition of Criticism—an announcement that the critic has stopped learning.

Facts are meaningless without purpose. The trustee of a financially troubled college told me of a board meeting where the cost of food service was bitterly debated. "No one could agree on the right way to figure costs," he said. "Can you tell me?" I responded by asking the purpose. Cash costs are what must be charged to break even for the short run in cash flow. Incremental costs are those involved in providing for a specified additional number of students. Full costs including depreciation and a share of general administration must be paid by someone in the long run. "So you do not know either," the trustee interrupted, and then he repeated that all he wanted was simple, impartial, objective facts so he could make the decisions for which he had the authority.

Facts exist in complex patterns, dimensions, combinations, and projections. The cost of food may include "service" that students do not need at times they do not want it. Workers may be able to provide alternatives that better meet diverse tastes or ethnic requirements. If decisions are made without getting the facts from students, workers, suppliers, health professionals, and administrators, there is little chance of maximizing either acceptability or productivity.

A number of accountants in establishment organizations have told me that when they are asked for data, they have difficulty finding the purpose or are denied it. One would expect those accountants to drift into the attitude that what is not worth doing is not worth doing well. In general, facts are unreliable if provided by those who are not involved in their use and do not find them meaningful. To be reliable, facts must be challenged for reasonableness in terms of purpose, tested for completeness in terms of sources or viewpoints, and finally integrated, reconciled, and interrelated.

If people are accepted and included, facts become available.

Negotiating

This is the adult-to-adult process of reaching agreement on some mutual undertaking. It is hindered by concepts and emotions rooted at the Authority level in the Established Organizational Model. First, negotiating is viewed as a weakening of authority. Second, it is believed to be necessary only for dealing with hostilities, antagonisms, and conflict. Third, it is thought to require compromising of principles and legitimate interests. Fourth, it is believed to involve techniques or skills which we need not learn and use ourselves. From this point it follows that we should allow or expect others to represent us, advocate our interests, and take care of us. But unless we negotiate we are children.

In the Established Organizational Model, work is structured in terms of decisions and authority. Thus Simon's *Administrative Behavior*[1] is subtitled *A Study of the Decision Making Process in Organization,* and its contents describe how behavior is shaped to fit the hierarchical model. And thus the college trustee referred to in the preceding section on fact finding sought neutral cost data on food service so he could use it in making decisions. In sharp contrast, work and information in the Target Organizational Model are structured by consensus. Consensus is shaped and defined by negotiation.

Effective negotiating is based on preparation, not tricks. Facts have to be assembled, needs determined, options and consequences explored. The initial presentations during a negotiation serve to set the tone and to educate as to needs and aspirations. To be successful in arriving at a consensus, we must focus on issues in all discussions, not on personalities. Focus on personalities creates an outcome in which there are winners and losers. Losers become reluctant workers and winners must then divide their efforts between working and enforcing their victory.

When the idea of compromise is introduced into negotiation, it is on the assumption that the parties have adverse interests and a gain for one is a loss for another. Any solution, therefore, must be reached by a series of trade-offs and concessions with the extent of each party's concessions being determined by bargaining skill and underlying power. In simple situations like a dispute between a taxpayer and a tax examiner over allowable depreciation rates, the settlement may be reached by compromising. But compromising like that is not an organizational process.

At the Fusion level, it is assumed that organizations should be synergistic. Negotiating at that level, therefore, is the process of arriving at an arrangement in which both individuals and the organization are moving toward their goals. The process is facilitated by distinguishing between needs and wants and between short-range and long-range goals. On the surface the results of negotiating and compromising may seem similar, but there is an essential difference which the parties feel.

COORDINATING

In the Established Organizational Model, coordination is achieved by telling people where to go, what to do, and how or how much to do it; or alternatively and perhaps as frequently, by telling people where not to go, what not to do, and how or how much not to do it. Those who do the telling are variously called administrators, instructors, leaders, or managers. Their interest is in perquisites, compensation, survival, and the efficient achievement of their spoken or unspoken goals.

To administer means to dispense or dish out. Administrators in service organizations dispense things like justice, health care, credentials, paperwork, and last rites. Instructors furnish data, motivate, and indoctrinate. Political and military leaders influence, command, and show the way. Professional managers take charge, plan, make decisions, direct, influence, and evaluate. In exchange, people are expected to give their administrators, instructors, leaders, and managers things like homage, loyalty, money, and subservience. Looking at such low-level coordinative concepts and exchange payments, most of us would agree with the retired dean of Columbia University's Graduate School of Business that they offer little hope for producing improved productivity: "most of our cherished social institutions: universities, museums, hospitals and others . . . do not have . . . access to cost reducing productivity improvements."[2]

> At this writing the nurses in San Francisco's hospitals are on strike, asserting there is more to nursing than being hand-maidens to doctors, more to health care than medical administration. And the nurses are being heard. Also at this writing the truancy rate in the Newark, New Jersey, public schools has passed the 50 percent mark. Who is listening to the truants?

Coordinating Functions

An executive in the Target Organizational Model performs four coordinating functions: (1) facilitating consensus, (2) making decisions in the absence of consensus, (3) supplementing the work of others, and (4) helping others to lift their eyes from their daily work to review goals and methods.

Facilitating Consensus. To improve communication, the executive must listen only to talk about work, not about people. To improve confrontation and feedback, the executive must bring in those with assigned responsibility whenever their problems are brought to his or her attention by others. The executive must establish the practice of reverse routing, that is, of returning mistakes to their originators rather than reporting them up the hierarchy for brownie points. These steps require effort, and they are not the way the established system works. At the Physical Force level, prison officials and police rely on informers. At the Authority level, officials of schools and other service organizations rely on confidential references, rating reports, and private grapevines. At both levels such communications have low reliability and can be used only for ranking and rejecting people, not for improving work performance.

> A key employee came into my office and said, "Mr. Heaton, I hate to do this, but I think you ought to know about one of your staff." "Don't tell me," I interrupted. "I will not listen to anyone talk about you and I see no reason to listen to you talk about anyone else. Please leave."

> The internal auditor gave me a two-page memorandum on how a policy set by a supervisor could be improved. The memorandum had not been reviewed with the supervisor. "What do you want me to decide?" I asked. "That you are brighter than the supervisor? That the supervisor should be demoted and you should take charge? That I should set the policies? Go talk with Eng and see if he finds your ideas valid. Report to me only on the financial controls for which you are responsible. Take your memorandum with you when you leave."

If executives in the Target Organizational Model do not use informers, stoolies, auditors, consultants, and psychiatrists to tell them about their people, how on earth can they know what's going on? The answer is simple. Their people tell them whatever they need to know because there is no need to cover up. There is a law of physics that for every action there is an equal and opposite reaction.

Thus in the Established Organizational Model, covering up and using informers are reciprocal systemic processes.

Along with disclosure of the Army's attempts to cover up My Lai and the Air Force's attempts to conceal the bombing of Cambodia came disclosure that the Army carried out illegal surveillance against American civilians and that the Navy was receiver of documents stolen from the National Security Council. Along with disclosure of the Watergate coverups and certain covert activities of the CIA came disclosure of spying against the American people by the White House Plumbers and of massive surveillance by the CIA. Secretary of the Army Callaway explained that when one man gets involved a little bit he starts trying to cover his tracks, and it just goes on and on. So to move away from spying and coverups toward organization by consensus, let people get accepted a little bit and step by painful step organizations will be changed.

As we have seen, facts are meaningless without purpose. To facilitate fact finding, therefore, it must be clearly stated that the facts are to be used for the purpose of improving the organization, not for ranking or punishing individuals. "No one will be blamed or punished for a mistake," I have said, "but any failure to learn from a mistake and to help others learn from it will not be tolerated." It took a while, but I learned to live with those words and adhere to them strictly. Step by step we have found both the facts and the maturity we need.

Making Decisions in the Absence of Consensus. At the lower levels in the Hierarchy of Organization Methods there are discrete acts, and at the higher level there are processes. Thus at the Physical Force level, loving is an act, and at the Fusion level, it is a process of daily living. In the Established Organizational Model, decision making is an act. In the Target Organizational Model, decision making is a process; like the hypotheses of scientists, decisions are formulated, tried, tested, reviewed, and modified in a never-ending cycle. And in the Target Model arriving at a consensus is a process, not an act. If the integrity of the process is maintained, there will be no decision making in the absence of consensus (see Figure 5-3).

Supplementing the Work of Others. Productivity of individuals or teams is not built on expectations of overall perfection. Skilled carpenters, clerks, lawyers, parents, surgeons, teachers, typists, and wine makers anticipate problems, find errors, make wrong guesses, and then adjust or correct to achieve their goals. Successful organisms convert weaknesses to strengths, as shown by athletes who have achieved excellence in fields where they had been weak or handicapped. Similarly, successful organizations of the Target Model develop strengths instead of treating weaknesses as permanent and exploiting strengths which already exist. In other words, successful organizations of the Target Model achieve a changing dynamic balance in which the work of each person toward personal and group goals is supplemented by the work of others.

Supplementing is not the same as giving a hand, doing again, doing for, or double checking. Compensating for weaknesses in one person by strengths in another is not part of the concept. The essence is that each person has a role which matches his or her competence and within which he or she is completely responsible. By fitting these roles (which change) like pieces of a jigsaw puzzle into the total organization (which also changes), the work of one person effectively supplements the work of others. Changes in roles are made currently and prospectively in the light of changing workloads and skills by a coordinator responsible for personnel and scheduling. The coordinator tries to respond rather than to initiate, seeking a consensus instead of making a decision. The coordinator's job does not exist in the Established Organizational Model, but it is one of the most important jobs in the Target Model.

> As a young auditor I was told not to waste my time checking things that were right. It was an instruction that puzzled me for years. Then I learned to visualize the roles and responsibilities of people in organizations that I audited. Like magic I could anticipate where most problems would be found. If I tell you that before I joined the Foundation, hiring for the comptroller's office had been on the basis of high school diplomas and typing skills, you will know what competencies there were in the accounting areas of budgeting, internal auditing, taxes, systems, and financial reporting. And you will know what initial supplementing was required.

Supplementing is the fitting of changing work roles to changing work goals. By matching work roles with attained skills, the coor-

FIGURE 5-3
Consensus Decision Guidelines
Some don'ts and dos.

DON'TS

1. Do not vote. Voting will split the group into "winners" and "losers" and encourages "either-or" thinking when there may be other ways. Voting will foster argument rather than rational discussion and consequently harm the group process.

2. Do not make early, quick, easy agreements and compromises. They are often based on erroneous assumptions that need to be challenged.

3. Do not compete internally. To reach a consensus either the group wins or no one wins.

DOS

1. Listen and pay attention to what others have to say. This is the most distinguishing characteristic of successful teams.

2. Try to get underlying assumptions regarding the situation out into the open where they can be discussed.

3. Encourage others, particularly the quieter ones, to offer their ideas. Remember, the team needs all the information it can get.

COMMENTS

When your group reaches the point where each person can say, "Well even though it may not be exactly what I want, at least I can live with the decision and support it," then the group has reached consensus. This doesn't mean that all of the group must completely agree, but rather that everyone is in fundamental agreement.

Since any team member can block a decision if he chooses, the approach suggested here is more difficult than other decision methods. However, it also tends to be more effective because it can force the team to consider more aspects of the problem and be more alert to objections to possible courses of action. Therefore, treat differences of opinion as a way of (1) gathering additional information, (2) clarifying issues, and (3) forcing the group to seek better alternatives.

Source: From training material prepared by the National Center for Dispute Settlement of the American Arbitration Association.

dinator facilitates responsible performance and keeps the focus on work, not personalities.

Helping Others Lift Their Eyes from Their Daily Work to Review Goals and Methods. When we do something we tend to focus on performance, not objectives, and the greater our concentration, the narrower our focus. Ask computer programmers if something can be done and they tend to respond in terms of programming steps without considering objectives or system alternatives. But no one with special knowledge should accept a question literally, because without the special knowledge, the question could not have been properly framed. Ask a tax accountant if home offices are deductible and a simple answer will be useless. Ask a doctor if ice packs are good for headaches and a simple answer could be dangerous.

Physical goods can be produced repetitively, and the harder one works the greater the output; the user of physical goods consumes them. Knowledge need not be produced repetitively for each user, and the user of knowledge does not consume it. But knowledge must be relevant, so the knowledge worker must know the purpose for supplying information. Similarly, the worker in a service organization must look beyond technology to the needs of the people being served. Knowledge workers can be effective only if they keep objectives in the fore. They must work smarter, not just harder.

The focus in service organizations should be to minimize routine activities, not to perform them more efficiently. For example, a checklist should be prepared by the benefits administrator to cover routine matters when an employee retires so sufficient time is available to deal with important matters like selection of an annuity option, beneficiary designations, tax problems, the possibility of a trust, and so on. The executive should facilitate working smarter. "Why are you doing this? Is it necessary or just helpful? Where is it on your priority list? If it is just a chore or meaningless routine, have you any ideas how it can be eliminated?"

To improve productivity for people, organizational stress must be on objectives rather than procedures, on responsibility for achievement of purpose rather than achievement of efficiency in turning something out.

PROGRESSION

Me
Me and Them
Us and Them
Us

CONCLUSION

At the Fusion level we have progressed to "us," signifying acceptance and inclusion of people in our organization. From this viewpoint we focus on work, work objectives, work problems, and work methods. In Chapter 7 we will explore how organizations can maintain the "us" position in hiring, assigning, and firing. But before that we will look in Chapter 6 at what we can do when an organization treats us as "one of them."

NOTES

[1] Herbert A. Simon, *Administrative Behavior: A Study of the Decision Making Process in Organization,* The Free Press, New York, 1957.

[2] Courtney C. Brown, "Inflation: The Dangerous Sedative," *Saturday Review,* Mar. 6, 1971, p. 22.

SIX

Deflecting Organizational Garbage

Once in a while when things are going badly, I reflect that most of the things I was blamed for have been the fault of others and most of the things that were good have been ignored or scorned. Such periods of self-indulgence involve regressing to a lower level of behavior in the Hierarchy of Organization Methods. Escape by the sword and be caught by the sword. Excuse oneself from blame at the Authority level by blaming others and thereby sanction the processes of ranking and rejecting in the Established Organizational Model. Exempt oneself from responsibility at the Influence level because everyone is doing it or because one person alone is nothing and thereby yield to the influence processes of conditioning, degrading, and introjecting.

We deflect nothing by regressing, sanctioning, or yielding. Nor by criticizing and judging. Nor by being hostile, aggressive, passive, dependent, indifferent, inhibited, or weak—each of which involves deprecating oneself and others. We deflect by moving up the Hierarchy of Organization Methods. Organizations are not homogeneous, but composite aggregations of separate and diverse transactions and interactions. Surprisingly, individuals have considerable power to determine the level of their own interacting and their own actions, transactions, and reactions in organizational composites.

No form of organization exists wherein personal satisfactions are automatic for anyone—of any rank. In fact, the presidents of organizations may feel put down, depressed, and helpless more

FIGURE 6-1

Not Interacting

Institutions as well as individuals can be unresponsive
and irresponsible unless made to change.

A conversation with Ivar Lovaas about self-mutilating children
and how their parents make it worse.

Lovaas: Trust your data; go where it takes you. Skinner's
contribution is chiefly methodological—he asks that
we find out what effect something has and act
accordingly, rather than assume that it works because a theory says it ought to.

Chance: You are saying that Skinner's contribution is in
identifying how to get control over the behavior
of the researcher and the therapist, not the pigeon.

Lovaas: Exactly . . .

I think a lot of people are doing this now, relying
more on empirical evidence than on a theory or a
great man. There are no great men around any more.
We don't have to have someone tell us where the
truth is any more; we look for ourselves. The day
of the great man in psychology is over, and I love
it. I think it is just great.

You know, you can get so obsessed with the great
men and the great theories that you end up hiding

in thought. You spend so much time intellectualizing that you don't get anything done.

Chance: One of the characteristics of autistic kids is that they get preoccupied with some behavior like rocking and they never get anything done. You are suggesting that many therapists and academicians are self-stimulating. They are so preoccupied with their theories and sand castles that . . .

Lovaas: That they never get anything done. Yes. What maintains and shapes them is not what they do in the external world but what they do in their own internal world. . . . And they will not do anything that has any impact on their society unless they are made to change. Any institution which isn't made accountable—a church, a government, a business—will self-stimulate.

Source: Paul Chance, "After You Hit a Child, You Can't Just Get Up and Leave Him; You are Hooked to That Kid," *Psychology Today*, January 1974.

often than the lowest members. Teachers may be assaulted by more garbage than students. And there are probably more parents than infants who are fatigued and abused. Organizations facilitate or obstruct, but individuals can establish considerable control over their satisfactions and aspirations and over the levels of method and process by which they seek to attain them.

STIMULI AND INTERACTING

The real action, Alinsky said, is in the reaction.[1] And experiments show that "what is learned in complex perception may relate more to the performance of responses than to the initial brain analysis of stimuli."[2] Thus interacting with the environment is essential for development because we learn more from seeing what we do than from passive seeing. Writers and accountants learn their trades through the point of a pencil. We all learn to walk or drive by trying and practicing with sensory feedback.

Not Interacting

There are individuals who decline to interact. They reject and exclude by dropping out, tripping out, tuning out, and turning off. Using alcohol, apathy, hard drugs, self-concern, and tranquilizers, they try to find their satisfactions in a single state of isolated consciousness which screens out unpleasant perceptions and eliminates the burdens of responding. In doing this they are not unlike those Established Model Organizations which restrict themselves to limited planes of perception and response wherein they can achieve esoteric profits or excellence. Ivar Lovaas, a psychiatrist, has noted that both autistic children and inward-looking organizations are self-stimulating (see Figure 6-1). Responding outwardly and interacting are necessary both for an individual to develop and for an organization to function productively.

In *The Natural Mind*, Andrew Weil[3] develops the thesis that there is an innate human need for variety in states of consciousness: sleep and wakefulness, action and reaction, low and high, straight and stoned, living in the present yet looking to the future, openness and receptiveness at all levels instead of closure at many or most. But in the United States today there are those who live mostly in a single state of closure or semiclosure. If Established Organizations have rejected and excluded one-third of the individuals in our society, perhaps a similar percentage of individuals have screened out environmental stimuli and live with minimal interaction.

Misery turns inward while exuberance reaches out. Shutting the world out by closing ourselves in makes us our own jailers. Being mere spectators or passive victims makes us senile when we are old and retarded when we are young. Not interacting, we deflect nothing and deny development to ourselves.

Playing Established Games

Games consist of rules for reacting to stimuli, and usually the rules are structured to create a contest or competition. Players are expected to react only to defined stimuli and only according to the rules. By concentrating, good players block out distractions, which means they reject stimuli from outside the prescribed structure of the game. By practicing, players improve their reactions, which means they develop those skills, physical and mental, which the game requires or permits.

Physiologically there is no difference between pleasure and pain (see Figure 6-2). To paraphrase, one person's drink is another person's poison, and beauty is in the eye or ear of the perceiver. But such diversity is unacceptable in playing games. A basic concept in games is that game rules provide the interpretation of stimuli. Thus players can be signaled either to start or stop by the same bell, whistle, or siren. And the distinction between rewards and penalties, moving the ball one way or another, is in the rules, not in the intrinsic nature of the stimuli. Finally, the distinction between success and failure, winning and losing, is in the rules and not in the intrinsic nature of the outcome.

A second basic concept in games is that behavior can be controlled by a graded scale of stimuli in the form of rewards and penalties. Where a little penalty does not dissuade, more penalty is called for. Penalties are designed to fit the infraction, and the ball is moved further when the infraction is defined as more serious. Oddly enough, this approach may teach players to break rules and risk penalties when they believe it will help them to win, and it

FIGURE 6-2
Interpreting Stimuli and Outcome

Individuals choose and control their interpretations.

The essential difference between the Read and Lamaze methods of prepared childbirth is this—Dr. Read believed that all that is necessary to remove pain is to remove fear and the tension that results from it. The Lamaze method recognizes the importance of this, but its main principle is based on the fact, well known to psychologists, that pain actually exists in our consciousness only as it is interpreted as such by the higher brain centers. These centers act like an infinitely complicated switchboard; they can handle only a certain number of incoming and outgoing messages at any given moment and block out all others that would distract or interfere. Applied to the problem of pain this means that just as it is possible for an athlete, his whole attention focused on running his race, to cut his foot and be unaware of the injury or of any sensation from it, so it is possible for a woman in labor, concentrating on doing a certain type of breathing which has become associated in her mind with the stimulus of the uterine contraction, to block from her consciousness the sensations which would otherwise accompany that contraction and be registered as pain.

From a paper read by Dr. Heinz L. Luschinsky in 1962 at the First International Congress of the Society for Psychoprophylaxis in Obstetrics.

*   *   *

General anesthesias had always left me vomiting, and at sea on a minesweeper during World War II, I was seasick much of the time. Andrew Weil's book *The Natural Mind* had a section on anesthesia and it included a comment on the delight of children in spinning until dizzy. I had never been delighted with dizziness and wondered why I had chosen to dislike the sensation.

Faced with a minor operation after reading Weil, I wondered if I could find dizzy pleasure in the anesthesia. The injection in the hospital room started the walls moving and I floated feeling buoyant. After the operation, I drifted in and out of consciousness with relaxed awareness. There was no nausea.

*   *   *

We who lived in concentration camps can remember the men who walked through the huts comforting others, giving away their last piece of bread. They may have been few in number, but they offer sufficient proof that everything can be taken from man but one thing: the last of human freedoms—to choose one's attitude in any set of circumstances, to choose one's own way.

Source: Victor E. Frankl, *Man's Search for Meaning*, Washington Square Press, New York, 1963.

leads administrators to escalate penalties in response to or reprisal for continuing violations. Players who conscientiously abide by game rules for interpreting life are described as "nice."

A third basic concept in games is that players don't set the rules. They are told what to respond to and how to respond. A fourth concept is that contests are usually "zero sum games." They produce nothing because every plus or gain for one player or side is offset by a minus or loss for the opposing player or side. Finally there is the concept that "the battle of Waterloo was won on the playing fields of Eton."[4] In other words, it is assumed that playing games prepares for life.

It can be observed that most game-playing concepts apply to the operations of hierarchies of authority. Confronted with the complexities and vastness of the world, the Established Organizational Model internalizes its purpose (e.g., making profits or being a good prison), defines its boundaries in terms of buildings or other internal criteria, and creates its own rules for interpreting stimuli and outcome. It is reassuring to an organization when other organizations adopt similar rules, because this extends the range of apparent order and stability. It is part of the pattern to have uniform examinations, such as college entrance examinations, for potential members of organizations and uniform rules, such as rules of war, for interorganizational dealings.

Fortunately for people, it may be true that game playing is as good a way as any for achieving certain aspects of personal development. Therefore, students, employees, prisoners, patients, and others in hierarchical organizations can interact as if playing a game and concentrate on developing those skills, physical and mental, which the game requires or permits. To accept games as reality, however, is self-destructive. Life is not a game and the interpretation of stimuli and outcome provided by the rules of a hierarchy of authority must be accepted only in game context (see Figure 6-2).

Playing Personal Games[5]

If one chooses to live by rules playing games, there are obvious advantages to making up one's own rules. One can thereby find victory in what the establishment interprets as defeat. But validation of personal rules is necessary and calls for assembling other players who will use the rules to interpret stimuli and outcome. In the game of Alcoholic, for example, the rules are used by drinker, rescuer, persecutor, and patsy and form a bond between them which in its place is perhaps as important as any other social bond in any other place.

In established games like baseball, players change positions and shift from field to bat, from offense to defense, and back again. So also in personal games like Alcoholic, players change positions from addict to ex-addict rescuer, from patsy to persecutor, from offense to defense, and back again.

At the level of reality, an individual will ask for help to solve a problem. At the personal game level one will ask for help not to solve a problem, but to reassure oneself of one's own worth. Playing the game Eric Berne called "Why Don't You—Yes But," the troubled individuals reassure themselves by showing that no one else can solve their problems. At the reality level the problem and alternative solutions are the focus. At the game level the focus is on emotions—the player with a problem wins not by finding a solution to the problem, but by putting down those who try to help.

> Harried Foundation Accountant: "Now the president is giving a speech so right away she wants total grants to foreign universities since 1961. With my workload it will be two weeks before I can get that information unless she wants the payroll to go out late."
>
> Associate: "Can't you get yearly totals out of the published annual reports?"
>
> Harried Foundation Accountant: "Yes, but the annual reports show payments, not grants awarded."
>
> Associate: "Can't you use payments and convert them by adding the current balance in unpaid grants?"
>
> Harried Foundation Accountant: "Yes, but we won't know that balance until we post at the end of the month."
>
> Associate: "Why don't you use the balance at the end of last month? Isn't that available?"
>
> Harried Foundation Accountant: "Yes, but she asked for up-to-date figures."

Associate: "Can't you estimate the current month or round off to the nearest thousand dollars?"

Harried Foundation Accountant: "Yes, but we are supposed to be accurate, not to go around making things up."

Associate (*conceding*): "Well anyway, I sure hope you get the payroll out on time."

The essence of personal games can be described as converting real problems into people problems. Playing "Why Don't You— Yes But" will not put bread on the table, change a flat tire, or produce an accounting report. Neither will it help an individual to develop skills and achieve confidence. Self-development requires that personality or people problems be converted into work problems. "In fact," wrote Andrew Weil, "the ability to forget oneself as the doer seems to be the essence of mastery of any skill."[6]

Acting Out a Script[7]

If the world is a stage, not an arena, then people are actors acting out scripts, not players playing out games. And there are advantages to choosing or identifying the personal script one wants to live by or for which one is predestined. Having chosen a personal script, the actor can move through the complexities and vastness of the world alert for cues, ignoring extraneous stimuli, and using predetermined gestures, words, and moves.

What more can be asked of people but that they act their age and script? Nothing, of course. Actors short-change themselves, not others. Although acting out, like playing personal games, involves duplicity and pretense, it is the actors themselves who pay the price for their self-deception. Established Organizations ask of their workers nothing more than that they act their assigned parts. Individuals can ask more of themselves, and individuals must answer to themselves.

Interacting progresses through three consecutive stages: (1) initial stress or fear, (2) testing or orienting responses, and (3) exploration and enrichment. Behavior in all three stages may be observed in a short time span when a one-year-old child encounters a strange adult (or vice versa). Movement from one stage to another is not automatic, however, and may never occur. Stress or fear may inhibit orienting responses and result in withdrawing instead of interacting. Orienting responses may be ineffective or counter-productive, as in the cases of playing personal games and acting out personal scripts; both confine the individual to stage two until they are abandoned.

PURPOSE AND INTERACTING

In the Established Organizational Model they say that behavior patterns emerge only from environmental and hereditary sources. At the levels of Physical Force, Authority, and Influence, B. F. Skinner[8] finds that purpose is extrinsic to people and *sui generis* only to the perception model for which he sees and speaks. It is the Established Organizations, the argument goes, which convert people's random activities into cooperative efforts and ac-complishments. But to argue that human behavior is externally controlled or conditioned, or even that it should be, tells us more about the viewpoint of the observer than it does about the devel-opment of people. As we now know, purpose has no place in the Established Organizational Model, but belongs to the privileged few near the apex of the hierarchical pyramid.

Control of purpose is control of power. In purpose is the power of an individual to achieve, to perceive beauty, to subordinate pain, and to interact at the stage of exploration and enrichment. Just as rules are at the heart of the Established Organizational Model, purpose is at the heart of the Target Model. Without purpose an individual cannot move up the Hierarchy of Organization Methods to the levels of Fusion and Development.

What Objectives Do

If I throw stones aimlessly into a lake, I can neither appraise my accuracy nor improve it. If I study without an idea of what I will do in the future, I can appraise neither the relevance of what I am learning nor the sufficiency of my mastery. Short-range objectives control interpretations of current stimuli and reactions as when throwing stones at a target. Long-range objectives provide a struc-ture and perspective for interpreting stimuli and directing efforts through cycles of activity. Indeed, long-range objectives may control the cycles.

Without objectives, we do as we are told during periods of organized activities and aimlessly pass the time between such periods. Without objectives, we seek to avoid effort, fatigue, and stress. Our release of energy without purpose, as in vandalism, develops no skills. Our blind adherence to rules and procedures, as in a bureaucracy, develops no judgment. Our sublimation of energy, as in drinking, watching television, or finding fault with others and the system, improves nothing in our lives.

Of course, we need some time which is not controlled by rules or purpose. Free time permits reinterpretation of both stimuli and outcome and that is what reflection and re-creation are all about.

Relinquishing objectives changes work problems to personal problems. Without objectives, our happiness depends on how deserving the system finds us, how fate deals, and how nicely people treat us. With practiced sensitivity, most stimuli become aversive. Conversely, taking on objectives changes personal problems to work problems. How we are graded is subordinated to what we learn, what we are dealt is subordinated to how we play our cards, and how we are treated is subordinated to how we react. There is still suffering, but it tends more to frustration in doing than hurt in being done. And frustration in doing can be followed by satisfaction in achieving, while hurt can only fade.

Getting Objectives

How do we get objectives? At the Influence level they say, "Why bother, use ours," and then connive, condition, and introject to get us to do so. In the Established Organizational Model they naturally limit our objectives to their slots, then test to be sure our aspirations are realistic in their terms. At the Authority level they offer rules in place of goals, then test to see how well we'll play the game.

At the Fusion level they assume we are autonomous—Theory Y with independent objectives—and they say, "Let us arrive at a consensus on what we do and how we do it, in the light of our objectives and of yours." How do we get there? How do we get the objectives that the Target Organizational Model assumes we have?

There is really no big mystery. We get objectives by paying for them, and the currency in which we pay is effort, sweat, and striving. From the moment of birth an infant strives: strives to eat, to see, to grasp, to roll over, to crawl, to stand, to walk, to run, to climb. When striving stops, objectives vanish, or more precisely they turn into dreams or even death. It seems clear that striving toward objectives can lead to competence, accomplishment, and personal effectiveness. It also seems clear that passivity and aimlessness can lead only to incompetence, lack of accomplishment, and personal ineffectiveness. Martin Seligman[9] asserts that psychological depression is really the belief in one's own helplessness; in other words, belief in one's inability to strive for one's own objectives (Figure 6-3).

> I once taught a course called "How to Make It on Your Own, Running a Business, Selling Your Services" to a group of inmates in a maximum-security prison. Observing six students who are now my friends, I learned how each strove toward his objectives:
>
> G. conceded the system its turf, did craft work in his cell at night, and used his products to interact at a different level.
>
> H. arrived at a consensus with the system, working on prison records toward his job goal on release (bookkeeping and accounting).
>
> K. took the system's garbage without complaint as his contractual due for wrongdoing; he saw it as paying his debt to society.
>
> R. held to his principles and asserted his rights regardless of punishment or harassment.
>
> S. changed his environment with humor, often inverting its perception of outcome.
>
> T. used a mixture of methods.
>
> Each found meaning in how he lived, not how he was treated. Each reacted effectively to the present processes of the system.

FIGURE 6-3
Helplessness Negates Purpose

To strive toward objectives, individuals need
some measure of power and control.

Lifesaving Self-Control. The staffs of hospitals, mental institutions, old-age homes, prisons, and other institutions are often
oblivious to the life-threatening effects of helplessness. The
usual doctor-patient, caretaker-aged, jailer-inmate relationship
fails to provide institutional inhabitants with a sense of control.
In hospitals, the doctor knows all; patients are expected to sit
back calmly and rely on the staff to make them well. While this
extreme dependency may be helpful to some patients, others
will not recover unless they can assume greater control over their
lives. In a physically or mentally sick person, loss of control may
be enough to tip the balance toward death.

Helplessness Tips the Scales. So, if a person or animal is in a
marginal physical state, weakened by malnutrition or heart disease, helplessness can push the scales towards death. One of the
most vulnerable groups to death by helplessness is the aged. In
America growing old is tantamount to losing control. Forced to
retire at 65, sent to an old-age home, ignored by relatives, the old
person is systematically stripped of control over his life. We kill
many of our senior citizens by denying them choices, purpose in
life, control over their lives. Many of these deaths are premature
and unnecessary.

Source: Martin E. P. Seligman, "Submissive Death: Giving Up on Life,"
Psychology Today, May 1974, p. 84.

Arriving at a Consensus

We have seen that the rules and activities of organizations in the Established Model are self-serving. As students, are we to submit to a school's demeaning dress codes, irrelevant subject require-ments, and Theory X teachers, or should we drop out? As teachers, must we be relentless task masters over Theory X students and become part of the system, or drop out? As school administrators, must we endure sit-ins and abuse from students and have our authority eroded by teachers' contracts, or drop out? Or can we build protective shields?

In these questions there are assumptions as to how we should react. First is the assumption that we should judge organizations and the people in them. But we can be caring only when we care, not when we judge. And organizations are living organisms too, worth caring for and with lives of their own like marriages and families. Second is the assumption that the alternative to submis-sion is to reject and drop out. But we can move up or down the Hierarchy of Organization Methods by ourselves without expect-ing an entire organization to move with us, and indeed it never can. Third is the assumption that striving is worthwhile only in an ideal environment where we are appreciated. But the personal consequences of striving are the same whatever our environment and so are the personal consequences of passivity.

Also in these questions there are assumptions as to the nature of rules. First is the assumption that rules are negative and restrictive, limiting our freedom and individuality. But if there is only one road and many people want to use it going both ways, freedom is gained, not lost, by arriving at a consensus to drive either on the left or right. Second is an assumption that arbitrary rules are undesirable. Whether a rule like driving on the right is seen as arbitrary or purposeful depends on the level from which we choose to view it. Third is an assumption that rules which symbolize belonging to an organization, like saluting or conforming to dress codes, are those to give priority to in our attention or complaints. Such rules in no way limit our striving, our objectives, and our values, in no way restrict our developing and achieving. To focus on such rules is to convert work problems to people problems. Here again our in-terpretation depends on the level from which we choose to view, and it is our interpretation, not the rule, that will assist or retard us.

The end is not to be independent and self-sufficient, although for years I thought it was. As a CPA in public practice I was bound by a code of ethics which required me to be independent. Professional independence, I learned, was based on competence and integrity and it was controlled by rules which, for example, prohibited me from having a financial interest in a company I audited. I can remember being proud of a superior in a dispute with a client. The client's comptroller made the dire statement that we just did not seem to see the issue the way he did. And my superior responded that if we always saw things his way we would be unnecessary. It was good training as far as it went.

Achieving independence is necessary before anyone can achieve interdependence. In union there is strength, but only between independent adults. A dependent can only take, not give. If achieving synergy can be viewed as a goal of organizations and society, it requires sharing the good and the bad, riches and deprivation, successes and failures, abilities and disabilities, sicknesses and health. Only by achieving independence can one move on to Fusion.

At the Fusion level, we accept and include and move toward a consensus. Responsibility for arriving at a consensus falls on individuals. The establishment can function at no higher level than its members, and in this sense, the input of those with low rank can be as important as the input of those whose rank is high. The processes of arriving at a consensus which were presented in Chapter 5 become part of the system only when we use them.

CONCLUSION

"No man is an island, entire of itself."[10] Since no one is complete and self-sufficient and since we know people by the way they reach out and know their goals by the way they strive, a proper study is of the methods and processes by which people reach out, strive, interact, and create organizations.

NOTES

[1] Saul D. Alinsky, *Rules for Radicals*, Random House, New York, 1972, p. 129.

[2] *Physiological Psychology: Readings from Scientific American,* with Introduction by Richard F. Thompson, W. H. Freeman & Company, San Francisco, 1972, p. 222.

[3] Andrew Weil, *The Natural Mind,* Houghton Mifflin Company, Boston, 1973.

[4] John Bartlett, *Familiar Quotations,* 14th ed., Little, Brown and Company, Boston, 1968. The quotation about the playing fields of Eton appeared in William Fraser's *Words on Wellington,* 1889.

[5] Eric Berne, M.D., *Games People Play,* Grove Press, Inc., New York, 1964.

[6] Weil, op. cit., pp. 35–36.

[7] Eric Berne, M.D., *What Do You Say After You Say Hello?,* Grove Press, Inc., New York, 1972.

[8] B. F. Skinner, *Beyond Freedom and Dignity,* Alfred A. Knopf, Inc., 1971.

[9] Martin E. P. Seligman, "Submissive Death: Giving Up on Life," *Psychology Today,* May 1974, p. 84.

[10] John Bartlett, *Familiar Quotations,* 14th ed., Little, Brown and Company, Boston, 1968; quotation attributed to *Devotions* by John Donne.

SEVEN

Accepting, Including, Discharging

Independent cells become interdependent in forming tissues. Independent tissues become interdependent in forming organs. Independent organs become interdependent in forming people. And independent people become interdependent in forming families, extended families, and other organizations structured on the Target Model. The entire progression is based on accepting and including. Along the way, symbiotic relationships are developed with other organisms like intestinal bacteria, domestic animals, trees, grasses, predators, and scavengers, adding up to our largest concept of organization, which is referred to as the balance of nature and which is based on accepting and including.

The sun revolves around us in the Established Organizational Model, so we administer or manage to achieve our own objectives without much thought for consensus. Based on processes of rejecting and excluding, our organizations reject more people as the organizations become more efficient in physical production, at least in terms of conventional measurements. But for organizations charged with rendering services, the methods and processes of the Established Model cannot work. Increased effectiveness in rendering services cannot be achieved by rejecting and excluding people.

Theory aside, let's get down to the nitty-gritty. The admissions office of an ivy league college triumphantly receives seven applications for every opening in the freshman class. So the staff gets down to work, eliminating and rejecting. Out go the letters to those rejected, suggesting they apply to another college with lower standards and requirements. There is no alternative to rejecting and excluding. Or is there?

ACCEPTING

There were people before there were organizations to reject them, and people built this country by cooperating and organizing. Now we state as axiomatic that in union there is strength, but we have progressed from Washington's army of citizens to today's army which rejects applicants and hands out administrative discharges by the tens of thousands.

Cooperatives as self-help organizations started becoming important in this country about one hundred years ago. Small farmers, small businesses, and consumers formed cooperatives to achieve collective strength in buying and selling. The usual association rules implied accepting: open membership, one vote per member, equal ownership, and dividends in proportion to patronage. By merger and consolidation, however, the number of farm cooperatives is now declining, their concept of self-help is being replaced by management, and their rules are changing to provide leverage to their more important members and to reject outright the weaker members who have the greatest needs.[1]

How strange that we have to learn again that accepting is possible and practical. Administrative efficiency is counterproductive in achieving productivity for people. How strange that we have to learn again how to accept.

Admissions

The Yale Arborvirus Research Laboratory is a major world center for virus research, maintaining, among other things, a reference set of arboviruses for use in identifying specimens sent in from remote field stations. There have been many applicants for the limited number of openings to study there, and my friend Dr. Charles R. Anderson served on the admissions committee. It seemed apparent that all applicants were acceptable, he told me, and there was no attempt to rank them. Instead the applicants' career plans and the places they intended to work were reviewed in terms of priorities in the worldwide virus research program and selection was on that basis. No applicant was downgraded, disrespected, or rejected.

Battlefield medical teams have developed the concept of triage for emergency treatment. The wounded are sorted into three groups: (1) those who will die even if treated, (2) those who will live even if not treated, and (3) those for whom treatment can mean the difference and who, therefore, are given priority. The triage concept involves accepting, not ranking and rejecting. It presents goals and challenges to the medical teams and leads to continuing improvement in performance. If instead of being accepted the wounded were ranked, attention would shift from medical performance to the ranking process. Based on the Fusion level process of accepting, it is not surprising that battlefield medical care has shown dramatic improvement in effectiveness.

The reciprocal relationship between accepting people and institutional change is seen in the City University of New York, which adopted an open-admission policy in 1970. In Manhattan Community College I saw change so rapid it was almost an upheaval: expansion, curriculum revisions, confusion, and instructional faltering and recovery, but also exciting educational advances and a yield which I harvested for the comptroller's office of first-rate student interns and two-year graduates. LaGuardia Community College, also part of the City University, was born after open admissions and has been remarkably innovative, establishing a work-study program for all students and reaching out to cooperate with other institutions such as the Lexington School for the Deaf. In sharp contrast, institutions which enforce the rejecting process, like our prisons and our warehouses for retarded children, remain essentially unchanged despite pressure, publicity, and management directives.

Hiring Interviews

Hiring to fill a slot in a hierarchical organization of the Established Model involves ranking and rejecting. Tests of personality, intelligence, and aptitude are used along with school grades to rank applicants. References are checked confidentially so they can say bad things about applicants behind their backs without embarrassment. The function of the interviewer is to shrewdly pick the best applicants, and applicants are expected to cover up their weaknesses and overstate their strengths. In other words, good hiring, like good justice in the Established Model, is conceived to be based on antagonistic sparring or what Thorstein Veblen has characterized as a spiritual attitude of animus.[2]

Hiring to fill a place in an organization of the Target Model involves seeking a consensus on objectives and needs. Applicants are accepted as individuals, and interviews focus on whether or not the job openings correspond to their present levels of skills, but still leave room for them to learn and develop. The function of the interviewer is not to select, but to define the nature and conditions of a relationship in which individuals and the organization can learn and develop together.

> On August 10, 1973, the Spanish American Training Institute sent us a nineteen-year-old male immigrant from El Salvador as an applicant for a job as a keypunch operator. The employment interview was fairly brief.
>
> "Let's see now," looking at the application form, "you have studied keypunching four weeks. How fast do you type? Do you think that is good enough? What do you think is a good standard and how long will it take you to get there? Will you take a typing course? Where? Do you have a typewriter or would you like to borrow one to practice on? What do you really want to do?
>
> "Did you know Manhattan Community College has a course in data processing? Would you be interested in their courses in English as a second language? Yes, that probably is the next priority after a typing course.
>
> "Are you the sensitive type? Okay, but let me tell you what I really mean. In this office we believe you should be told about your mistakes so you can learn from them. And if you make a really big mistake, we ask everybody else to look at it so they can learn from it too. We never talk about mistakes privately. Will you be comfortable with this approach?
>
> "Do you like to work? In this office we have no police. If you need someone checking up on you to get off the phone, this is not the place for you. If you run out of work, we expect you to ask, not sit around until someone notices.

"If we get an urgent job, would you be willing to put in overtime at night or work on Saturday?

"What can I tell you? You understand what is expected? If you want the job, when would you want to start? Okay. See you then."

Correlations

Accepting is a process, not an act, and day-to-day activities make up the process. By accepting, one gives responsibility; conversely, by exercising authority and directing, one dissipates responsibility and rejects. To act like an administrator and make administrative decisions is inconsistent with giving responsibility and accepting.

Theory X perceptions and behavior correlate with the day-to-day procedures of organizations structured on the Established Model. Thus the Theory X perceptions of a conventional teaching university correlate with the processes of ranking and rejecting which are intrinsic in its admission routines. Conversely, the Theory Y perceptions of an organization structured on the Target Model can only correlate with processes of accepting and including in its admission routines. On my first day in Union Graduate School, Goodwin Watson opened the colloquium by telling us where we would find our resources for learning: first, within ourselves as individuals; second, in our fellow students; and third, in the core and adjunct faculties. The Theory Y student body which Watson assumed and the learning behavior which he described could only exist in a student body emerging from admission processes that had defined the interdependencies involved in joining and participating.

Selection procedures designed to screen out Theory X individuals are incompatible with the perceptions and goals of responsible service organizations. And great innovative organizations like agricultural cooperatives and universities without walls which have goals of Fusion and Development will inevitably die out or be corrupted if their administrative procedures are those of Authority, Force, or Influence.

INCLUDING

Accepting and including is a process within our Target Model Organizations as well as at their borders. Similarly, in organizations of the Established Model, rejecting and excluding is a process within as well as at the borders. Consider a military organization and applicants to a military academy. Ranked by various conventional measurements, the lowest applicants are successively eliminated until the residue matches the number of openings in the first-year class. For those admitted to the academy, the process of ranking and eliminating continues until a reduced remainder is graduated. For those admitted to the corps of officers, the process of ranking and eliminating continues, with those passed over for promotion being forced to leave.

Somehow we have been socialized to see no alternative to the processes of ranking, rejecting, and excluding, but what we need to see is that these processes are nonproductive. Consider young adults thirteen through sixteen years of age. Excluded from jobs and without status or place in society at large, they are forced to attend school by being defined as criminals if truant. School thus becomes the alternative to internment in a correctional facility. But the conventional school itself employs the processes of ranking, failing, rejecting, and excluding. By law, however, the students who have failed and been rejected must be retained because there is no place to exclude them to. Can you visualize these typical schools and their students, mostly urban perhaps, but also suburban and rural? Now think about decision theory, information systems, grid analysis, management by objectives, and productivity measurements. Are they relevant to the problem? Do they offer hope of improvement? Or must the fundamental processes be changed? Is it time to reacquire some practical know-how in accepting and including?

Pressures

Some kind of pressure and tension is necessary if we are not to become jellyfish. Pressure for efficiency is part of the process of rejecting people. Pressure for responsibility is part of the process of accepting them. It can be observed that when there is pressure for efficiency, there is no learning or development. As John Dewey recognized early in this century, learning involves reflection on experience. Efficiency, on the other hand, is merely rapid repetition of what is already known.

Efficiency cannot be measured and pressured for in jobs like research, college teaching, diagnosing, and tax accounting, where learning is a major element. In production jobs, however, pressure for efficiency can squeeze out learning. Thus, for efficient keypunch operators, bank tellers, and assembly-line workers, there is no learning. Not at all coincidentally, efficient workers mostly have dead-end jobs with no career ladders available for advancement. In accordance with the laws of physics, administrative pressures, like other pressures, provoke equal and opposite antagonistic reactions. And from an administrative viewpoint, to complete the circle, jobs without learning time are seen to be filled mostly by Theory X people who must be pressured to produce.

Of course, perceptions are as much in the set and setting of the beholder as in the scene. Thus organizations, as well as individuals, can be identified as Theory X or Theory Y. Pressing for efficiency, the Theory X organization precludes its own learning and development. To lay standards and measurements on students involves freezing the curriculum, the teachers, and the school. Similarly, in the factory—where time-and-motion study experts set standards, cost accountants analyze variances and prepare exception reports, supervisors discipline and enforce efficiency, and harried administrators authorize and expedite—no one learns and the organization trades its future for the present, foregoing progress and development for the status quo.

But since pressure and tension are necessary if we are not to become jellyfish, some kind of pressure and tension must be created in the Target Organizational Model. What kind of pressure and tension is developmental? The answer is pressure of and for responsibility, although it can indeed be onerous and stressful. Responsibility requires the individual to be independent, but it is the nexus of interdependence. Strong authority is required to enforce responsibility.

Akin to responsibility, or the first stage of it, is accountability. As an accountant the concept has fascinated me, and I have found it widely applied and understood in business, widely denied and misunderstood in nonprofit organizations. To be answerable for what one does, one must first have objectives outside oneself, and we have seen that these are lacking in nonprofit hierarchies of authority. Too often the thrust in nonprofit organizations has been to deny not only commercial purpose or practicality, but any purpose of any kind. To improve the productivity of any organization, there must be unrelenting pressure for purpose, accountability, and responsibility. Evil in all its venality as seen by Hannah Arendt[3] is in the simple doing without regard to purpose or result.

Pressure in organizations should be for development. As seen in the behavior of infants, development involves a cyclical process of observing, striving, and reflecting. The pressure in the Target Model should be to enforce this cycle, because in organizations that deal in knowledge and service, we must work smarter, not just harder. Learning should be viewed as an investment—an investment in the future like any other investment. The return on learning and development as a continuing process is the highest available and must be pressured for against the temptation of achieving short-run efficiency by giving orders.

> In a dozen remote locations around the world, The Rockefeller Foundation has professional field staff working on projects in agriculture, education, and medicine in cooperation with local governments and institutions. The Foundation's presence is never permanent. Local professionals work with and are trained to replace Foundation personnel. Local personnel provide supporting services and perform all office functions. Twice during my tenure as comptroller, there were defalcations in field offices. In both cases a local accountant took the funds and left or fled after admitting guilt. In both cases the local branch of an international auditing firm had failed to discover the defalcation. In both cases there had been a breakdown of system and control which was obvious in retrospect.
>
> I visited both locations soon after the losses occurred, working with the auditors by processes at the Authority level and with the project staffs by processes at the Fusion level. Meeting with the auditors, we focused on the past, sought to blame, obtained some admission of possible inadequacies, and terminated their engagements. Talking with staff, we focused on the present and future, sought to define opportu-

nities for improvement, and obtained a consensus on skills to be developed and procedures to be improved. We accepted and included each other as partners in a continuing program.

"You ask what I think of your office operations, whether they are good or bad, satisfactory or unsatisfactory. There is no way to know or judge except to say that your operations cannot be developed beyond your personal knowledge and skills. Perhaps your operations are at the level of the New York office ten years ago, and there we have another ten years of improvements in mind. That means you have at least twenty years of personal growth and system development ahead. Now let's talk about priorities and what should be done next year. Shall we start with your ideas or mine?"

Giving immunity from being graded by my standards at the Authority level was only an invitation for the staff to move up the Hierarchy of Organization Methods. The cost of accepting the invitation then had to be stated and a payment schedule established. Staff members were asked to prepare signed reports at the end of every month giving their work status, backlogs, descriptions of open problems, and plans for improvement the following month. Staff members were made to understand that continuing improvement was a condition of continuing employment. Reversion to the Authority level by concealing mistakes or problems was defined as grounds for dismissal, but could perhaps have been explained better as a decision by the individuals to withdraw and exclude themselves. The pressure laid on the staff members was sobering but constructive because they were accepted and included.

Opportunities

In regard to opening a factory in Harlem, I heard the chairman of a great international corporation say he was in business to look for opportunities, not problems. And I heard the president of a famous university advise The Rockefeller Foundation to seek out the most attractive opportunities for its overseas programs. By opportunities both meant what any member of the establishment means.

In terms of the Established Organizational Model, an opportunity is a chance to strengthen and extend authority. At the lowest level, it is a chance to give an order telling someone what to do. Or it is a chance to authorize some act or payment and be superior. At a higher level, an opportunity is a chance to set standards or write laws and regulations. At this level a great delight is to be an intermediary, passing on words from above and free from both responsibility and grimy toil. At still a higher level, as seen from the viewpoint of the establishment, an opportunity is a chance to develop models and demonstrate how well we do things (with all our money, knowledge, and authority). The satisfaction here is that models and demonstrations can regulate complex patterns of present and future behavior and can even change entire cultures. An example is the development of models for the delivery of health care. I have seen them in the Philippines, in India, and in South America, but they are seldom replicated—talk about casting pearls!

The reason for failure from the viewpoint of the Established Organizational Model is always the same: human weakness. Get the best person as a leader and that person will get followers. But as Dr. Charles Smith, who heads the Foundation's program in Equal Opportunity has said, you have to respect before you can serve. And authority is always extended over Theory X people.

A sharply different picture is seen in terms of the Target Organizational Model. There an opportunity is simply a good problem to work on. And the organizational process is not to tell and show but to listen and respond. If 98 percent of the children born in a South American country are delivered by untrained, unlicensed midwives and there is high infant and maternal mortality, that is a good problem. The approach of the Established Organizational Model is to establish a rural health center with midwives at the bottom of the hierarchy tolerated only because replacements are not available, threatened with rejection if they do not follow orders, and excluded from the planning and direction of the center. The approach of the Target Organizational Model is to accept the midwives and include them along with mothers and prospective mothers in the planning and direction of an association structured to support their efforts and aid them in their personal development and improvement.

In regard to the problems of the people who have been rejected, the perception of Established Organizations must be to justify their rejection and continuing exclusion. Thus in city ghettos there can be no attractive opportunities for organizations of the Established Model, and ghetto self-help activities such as parent-directed schools must be impeded. Likewise, in rural areas, the system that has driven out medium-sized farmers must, of necessity, impede those who strive to take their places. Thus the extension specialist who is paid by the government to help small farmers tells them to cease their futile striving and look for factory jobs. On the other hand, the Established Organizations can support leadership training among the rejected and excluded, because this defines the problem as a people problem, implies weaknesses in the system's victims, and diverts attention from those methods and processes of Established Organizations which might otherwise be exposed to challenge.

Failures, mistakes, and violations are intrinsic perceptions of superiors in the Established Organizational Model. Tell students what and when they must learn and they can fail. Eliminate the time limit and they cannot fail, but concurrently Authority must be replaced as the primary method of organization. Authority needs standards for enforcing and needs measurements of actual or potential failures for ranking, rejecting, and excluding. In order to move an organization up the Hierarchy of Methods, therefore, we must change our perception of failures, mistakes, and violations, change our reactions to them, and restrict their burgeoning creation.

Assuming Theory X people, the law exacts penance for mistakes and failures. The sword of justice is wielded not to achieve good ends, but to deter violations. Assuming Theory Y people, science redefines mistakes and failures as profitable experiments. The method of science is applied not to deter failures, but to achieve good ends from them. Not surprisingly, crime and violence have increased as hierarchies of authority have increased in size to encompass more of their Theory X people. Not surprisingly, the successes of science have increased as more people have learned to assert its method and apply it.

In perceiving errors, we must learn to worry about too few as we do about too many. Skills develop from practice. When errors stop, learning and development stop too. Improvement is a process of striving, feedback, and adjustment, and this holds true for organizations as well as individuals. The problem is to adjust for errors and build on them.

> In Navy ordnance we were taught to straddle the target to find the proper range. Fire with the range set at 8000 yards and the splash is seen between us and the target. Deliberately over-compensate to 9000 yards and the splash is seen behind the target. From there on the process is to halve differences, firing next at 8500 yards. If splash is behind the target, decrease to 8250 yards. To attempt immediate perfection or demand it is a futile process and the target may never be achieved.

The method of Authority is self-limiting. With new rules for each new problem, rules accumulate and as a consequence violations and failures increase, taxing the capacity of enforcement agencies. With more people rejected and excluded, Force becomes the method of control over them. Opportunities for the system diminish, becoming more remote and more difficult to find despite advanced technologies and new theories of decision making, management, and modeling. But while such opportunities decline, there are good problems to be perceived and worked on close at hand, using the methods of Fusion and Development which involve accepting and including.

"But everything is transformed—and nothing is demanded of this experience, no religious or moral or intellectual presupposition, nothing but *acceptance*."[4]

Assignments

A review of what goes on in organizations shows that almost every action tends to move them up the Hierarchy of Methods or down, toward development of strength or toward its current exploitation, toward effectiveness in service or toward efficiency in output, toward responsibility in the Target Model or toward authority in the Established one, into the process of accepting and including or into the process of rejecting and excluding. An organization is molded by how it acts, not by the goals or values it espouses.

A job description that starts "Under the supervision of the senior clerk, the junior billing clerk will post from yellow copies of sales invoices . . ." is moving toward Authority in the Established Model. The process starts to change if a preamble is inserted which states, "The junior billing clerk is responsible for the billing of all factory shipments to customers," and then goes on to list some of the detailed procedures which are currently involved. Add a section on the learning opportunities the job entails although there are no published patterns to be followed that we have found. Then in lieu of an annual evaluation, ask the junior billing clerk to describe accomplishments over the past year and plans for personal development and job improvement during the coming one. At this point, movement is toward the Target Model.

> To help define on-the-job learning opportunities, we prepared a list of skills required in an accounting office (see Figure 7-1). Then, from a selected few, we asked for statements of plans and accomplishments. Interest was not high until the year we asked for such statements from all personnel. Suddenly there were things to talk about and plans and schedules to be prepared for getting goals accomplished.

> A keypunch operator wrote: *"My plans for next year* are to work in the different sections, so I can learn more about office work and about the Foundation and how it works all around the world. This will be very interesting for me because I will get more knowledge and I will be of more value to the Foundation. I also would like to write programs and learn more about computers and the different kinds of work that can be done on them. That's why I am enrolled at the BMCC taking Data Processing. *My plans for last year* were to go to school to study English and Data Processing; learn to punch and verify all the kinds of work; learn to run some work on the computer. *My accomplishments last year* were that I learned to keypunch and verify all the kinds of work. I learned to run some work on the computer, like daily vouchers, drafts, credit memos, general entries, 80/80 listings, write labels, compiling programs, tape dumps, reproduce cards and do sorting. I also learned to do the monthly computer log."

> The assistant supervisor of the appropriations section wrote: *"My plans for next year* are to continue my college education. I

FIGURE 7-1

Skills Required in an Accounting Office

These are all work skills that can be learned; none of them are personal traits. *(Shading indicates the skill content of jobs by job level.)*

Skills which can be learned

Job levels

No skills level 5 *Clerical level 4* *Accounting level 3* *Supervisory level 2* *Reporting level 1*

RECORDING

Writing
Calculating
Sorting
Storing (filing)

PROVING

Checking
Reconciling
Finding errors
Balancing, matching, etc.

REVIEWING

Valuation
Cutoffs
Completeness
Reasonableness

Skills which can
be learned

Job levels

COORDINATING

Planning and scheduling
Designing procedures
Initiating improvements
Obtaining flexibility
Instructing and training
Communicating

CONTROLLING

Comparing
Analyzing
Observing and counting
Calculating independently
Scanning

INTERPRETING

Understanding operations
Understanding accounting
Understanding organization
Understanding people
Classifying
Selecting
Integrating

see the computer as a tool to eliminate non-thinking jobs and, therefore, plan to continue analyzing procedures in my section with this in mind. I hope to learn more of what is happening in all sections in the Comptroller's Office in order to better understand the interrelationship between sections and to avoid duplication of efforts. *My plans for last year* were to continue my education at Queens College and also to be able to attend a computer programming course. I had also planned to improve my understanding of the operations in the Appropriations Section and how they could be improved in quality and efficiency. *My accomplishments for last year* were that I completed an additional ten credits toward my B.A. I spent more time on analyzing work procedures within the Appropriations Section and have consequently changed and made suggestions for changes in procedure and forms. I've spent more time on thinking out an assignment/problem rather than in just getting it off my desk. Although I have not had the opportunity to take a computer programming course, I have increased my understanding of computer functioning by attending meetings and having discussions with staff in the Systems Section. This has helped me to better envision the computerization of this section and prepare for its implementation."

The secretary to an assistant comptroller wrote: "*My plans for next year* are to continue my school with graduation forthcoming in June for an Associate Degree. After graduation, I intend to transfer to a four-year college and continue toward an undergraduate degree. This will help me with my duties and association at the Foundation. To continue to improve my skills as secretary and to continue to learn other phases of work in the Comptroller's Office. To learn administrative duties. *My plans for last year* were to work toward my Associate Degree at school and improvement in my present capacity at the Foundation, to attend computer school. *My accomplishments last year* were to complete an additional eight credits toward my degree. I worked and improved my shorthand and familiarized myself to some extent with the budget of the Foundation and helped to do the typing of said budgets. Also was introduced to an auditing project on which I worked."

An assistant chief accountant wrote: "*My plans for next year* are to continue developing in the Quantitative Analysis Field and make further progress toward a Masters Degree in mathematics. I expect to use the computer with Statistical and Linear Programming Methods working on the impact of inflation on our activities, analyzing medical statistics from our St. Lucia project, assisting with the proposed revision of the Pension Plan, etc. as per separate report. *My plans for last year* were to develop and use the techniques of Quantitative Analysis and Operations' Research in defining and organizing projects for computer processing for the Comptroller's Office and other Foundation offices, both programmatic and administrative. *My accomplishments for last year* were to get some statistical analysis work done on the computer. A number of active projects are in various stages of development. I am preparing a detailed status report."

DISCHARGING

A supervisor wrote: "*My plans for next year* are not much different from those for last and the problems are about the same. Perhaps next year, if things go well, there will be some time for training." Consensus ended. Development of strength replaced by current exploitation.

In our organizations, we must choose one or the other and act on our choice: development or exploitation, continuing improvement or imposed standards of efficiency, consensus or directives, the processes of the Target Model or the processes of the Established one. If our choice is for the Target Model, we must erect career ladders and they must be used for climbing, not standing on. When any rung on a ladder is permanently occupied, the ladder is blocked off for all. In the Target Model, therefore, we are obligated to deal with the static or alienated person who does not participate in its dynamic processes.

But the shorter our time span and the narrower our focus, the more simply we see cause and effect and the more decisively we can react to Theory X failures by rejecting and excluding. The longer our time span and the broader our focus, the more complexly we see processes and responses and Theory Y successes. There are plateaus in learning and rhythms in development, so progress is not always visible. If we choose to accept and include we must persist until we see and understand the full rhythms and cycles of development and must tolerate their downturns and regressions.

If we choose to accept and include people, our priority in dealing with failures must be to correct organizational flaws. For example, I once erected a career ladder from the position of librarian for computer tapes, to librarian of computer output too, and then to librarian of all comptroller's office reports and tax returns. The librarian welcomed the opportunity, but over the months nothing seemed to happen. Was it a typical case of the Peter principle[5] with someone being promoted from competence in a lower job to incompetence in a higher one? So it seemed, until I had to squarely face the issue of accepting or rejecting. Accepting forced me to look back at the career ladder and see its flaws. The development of plans, policies, and procedures for the library should have been assigned to the chief accountant with the librarian to assist and implement. The correction was then easy and successful.

Nonetheless, there are often occasions in any organization when the right step at the right time is not open on a career ladder. Where an individual is pushed too fast or held back too long or placed where no career ladder has been erected, it is better for the individual to leave the school or place of work, and it is also better for the school or the employer. Such separation need not be marked with animus, but can instead continue the process of accepting and including.

> "So your goals are much the same as last year. We have said before that someday you would outgrow your opportunities here. Has that day come? Think about it and let us know what you decide and what we can do. It will be to your advantage and to ours to resolve the present situation."

CONCLUSION

In the Established Model, superiors must make the hard decisions of rejecting and excluding: laying off workers to improve efficiency, failing students to maintain standards, creating unemployment to cure inflation, and killing to enforce the rule of law. But we cannot improve the productivity of organizations by leaving them unchanged and rejecting people. Besides, the real courage and real fun are in the Target Model: in the give and take and confrontations of accepting and including and in the meeting of the challenges that emerge therefrom for externalizing goals, changing structures, and improving the procedures by which our organizations serve or could be made to serve everyone.

NOTES

[1] Linda Kravitz, *Who's Minding the Co-op?* Agribusiness Accountability Project, Washington, D.C., 1974.

[2] Thorstein Veblen, *The Theory of the Leisure Class,* Houghton Mifflin Company, Boston, 1973, p. 24.

[3] Hannah Arendt, *The Human Condition,* Doubleday & Company, Inc., Garden City, N.Y., 1958.

[4] Paul Tillich, *The Shaking of the Foundations,* Charles Scribner's Sons, New York, 1948.

[5] Laurence Peter and Raymond Hall, *The Peter Principle,* Bantam Books, Inc., New York, 1970.

EIGHT

Joining, Participating, Leaving

Organized social structures seem to have been part of life since life began on earth: from protozoans to bees in hives, from schools of fish to flocks of birds or sheep. Individuality, on the other hand, seems to be of modern origin, and this chapter is concerned with both the methods of its achievement and the methods of its use.

Two simplistic perception models tend to control our ideas about organizational structure and individuality. First is the Established Hierarchical Model: the pecking order of chickens, apes, and humans. In this model, individuality is recognized as significant only in the leader at the apex of a pyramid. Institutions exalt leaders, not anonymous parts in subordinate organizational slots. In turn, wealth and prestige are conferred on those institutions which proclaim leaders by providing their credentials prospectively and their honors concurrently or retrospectively. Surely it is not from this perception model that we will learn to develop as individuals except as stereotyped leaders or winners. Surely it is not from this perception model that we will learn to recognize the remarkable productivity of teams of individual achievers.

The second perception model, that of Rousseau's natural man, sees individuality as thriving only outside organizations. Thus, living the good life in this model means rejecting the organizational rat race, returning to nature, enjoying simple pleasures, and acting out personal love instead of socialized aggression. Intensely pessimistic in the face of exploding populations and expanding organizational structures, this model foresees more and more to withdraw from, and less and less to withdraw to. Surely it is not from this perception model that we will learn interdependence and that no isolated individual is complete and self-sufficient.

"If I am not for me, who will be? If I am only for me, who am I for? If not now, when?"[1]

LAYERING

Animal cultures and societies are concerned with, among other things, obtaining nourishment, education, health care, and protection. For providing these essentials, animal societies, like human societies, have evolved concepts of private and community property and have formed family structures and tribal organizations. We should expect observations of animal behavior to confirm as a basic perception model our Hierarchy of Organization Methods. Further, we should expect observations of animal behavior to show that the organizations of higher, more complex animals involve all the methods in the hierarchy, superimposing them one upon another.

An alpha lion attains his position by Physical Force. He exercises his dominance by Authority derived from and backed by Force. He extends control over the pride by Influence and even his sleeping presence is sufficient to maintain law and order. But when it hunts, the pride is organized by Fusion, with coordination of its spread-out line of advance, with single-minded consensus on the target prey, and with all members of the pride accepted and included on the hunting team. And the success of the pride in hunting is based on continuing development of individual and collective skills; Robert Ardrey notes that when a fence was erected in an African game park, a lion pride quickly developed tactics to trap its prey against the fence.[2]

If the hierarchy of authority is essential, so also is the Target Model. If the role of authority cannot be denied, neither can the role of responsibility. If it is the hierarchy of authority that creates and maintains an organization, it is the Target Model that makes it function and improve. To view either model as complete and sufficient of itself is dangerously naïve. A Complete Organization must combine both models (see Figure 8-1).

FIGURE 8-1

The Complete Organization

Without a strong base of force and authority to support it, the Target Model collapses. In the Established Model the boss directs, supervises, enforces compliance, and otherwise controls. In the Target Model, the boss reviews, feeds back, enforces responsibility, and otherwise supports. In the Established Model the boss parcels out pieces of work. In the Target Model the boss coordinates work opportunities with work roles. Roles are discussed later in this chapter.

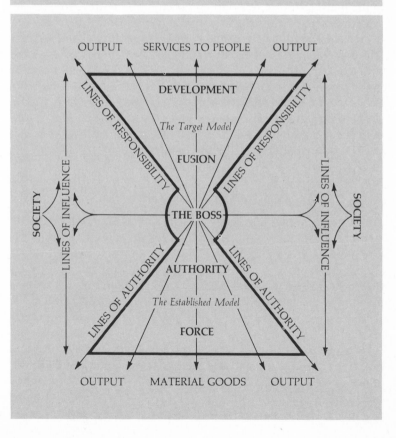

Zoo Behavior

Until recently, much of the academic knowledge of animal behavior was obtained from observations in zoos. But in a zoo there is no hunt and animals are cut off from purpose or striving. At the Fusion level, there can be no consensus on objectives and no coordinating of efforts. At the Development level, there are no skills to acquire and no learning to feed back. Thus the Target Organizational Model is nonexistent in zoos. The processes at the Influence level are obviously restricted—without a real animal society, for example, socialization has limited scope. And Authority can add relatively little to simple physical dominance.

There should be a predictable pattern to zoo behavior. Boredom, apathy, slothfulness, and preoccupation with sex are among the obvious expectations. So it should be no surprise that baboons exhibit outrageous sexual behavior in zoos. But in the last few decades there have been observations in the field in which we can find confirmation of our Hierarchy of Methods and how the methods are layered one on another and interrelated. In the wild, baboons are observed to have a complex society with many responsible roles for individuals, including those of elder statesmen. Examples have been reported of heroism and self-sacrifice which contrast sharply with zoo behavior.

Analogues for Zoos

There are analogues for zoos in which animals or people are cut off from purpose or striving and thereby are excluded from the methods of Fusion and Development. In such analogues we should expect to find a predictable pattern of zoo behavior. Thus the pecking order of barnyard fowl is focused on gratifications of the moment because without purpose there is no future. But in the wild we see game birds feigning injury to lead us away from their young.

In peacetime armies there is zoo behavior, but waging war requires shared goals and the methods of Fusion and Development. David Cortright in *Soldiers in Revolt*[3] carefully and laboriously assembled the Vietnam war statistics of desertion in American forces, dropping out with drugs, mutinies, fragging, sabotage, and just plain refusing to fight, all demonstrating anew that behavior engendered by the Established Organizational Model alone is ineffective in combat. Both military and political authorities had only one question—"How can we get *them* to do what we want?" A large military budget cannot assure the safety of America if its military and political leaders use an inadequate perception model of organizations and see fellow citizens as *them*, the problem.

It is easy to find other examples where authoritative management practices and theories are squeezing out the Target Model and engendering zoo behavior. Factory assembly lines are an obvious starting point. Restrictive bureaucratic procedures are another. Then there are dead-end jobs like packing and shipping in department stores. By precluding hope of future opportunity and satisfaction, dead-end jobs also preclude purposeful striving and engender zoo behavior. Schools which are structured as hierarchies of authority tend to become custodial institutions like zoos and prisons, but by definition and common sense, education can take place only in the Target Model at the Development level. And welfare recipients are seen as slothful and preoccupied with sex.

Zoo behavior is real, but it is mostly a reflection of organizational structure rather than of innate individual characteristics. This is shown by the way normal animals and people regress to zoo behavior when placed in a zoo setting. Wild animals when trapped and imprisoned in a zoo must regress to zoo behavior or die. Older people forced into uselessness after retirement become senile or die. Hospital patients in intensive care units, when merely controlled rather than supported, regress to zoo behavior or die (see Figure 8-2). And the converse is also true. Given meaningful roles at the Fusion and Development levels, children learn and mature, addicts dry out, senile oldsters function rationally again, and soldiers fight effectively (see Figure 8-3).

Renouncing or Denying

The Established Organizational Model is not a Complete Organization, but neither is the Target Model. A foundation without a superstructure is not a complete building, but neither is a

FIGURE 8-2

Regressing to Zoo Behavior

An illustration of how any of us can regress
when placed in a zoo analogue.

Any individual who finds himself dependent will respond in characteristic ways. The ICU patient responds to dependency with greater intensity than the usual surgical patient. Barker et al. have defined four features of regression secondary to dependency. These features are readily applied to ICU patients.

1. The patient becomes self-centered, like a young child, seeing himself as the center of his own solar system. He perceives all events in relation to himself and his benefit, even though reality may be to the contrary. His desire for gratification of every need becomes immediate and out of proportion.

2. His interest is circumscribed, and his attention is on the present moment only.

3. His emotional dependence on those around him is paramount, and he interprets their behavior in terms of rejection or acceptance of him. His moment-to-moment ambivalence is apparent.

4. Bodily function is his primary preoccupation.

Source: Marian J. Reichle, "Psychological Stress in the Intensive Care Unit," *Nursing Digest,* May-June 1975.

FIGURE 8-3
Reversing Zoo Behavior

An example of how regression to zoo behavior,
when understood, can be reversed.

Most disoriented, agitated, or hostile geriatric patients face a dismal future because so few health-care professionals believe these symptoms are reversible. Diagnosed as senile, senile psychotic, or as suffering organic brain syndrome, such patients are considered poor prospects for treatment and usually don't get any, except for custodial care. As totally dependent human beings, they usually end their days after long and pointless stays in psychiatric institutions. But such a pervasive pessimism among health professionals is not justified.

Elderly disturbed patients can be rehabilitated, and many can function quite independently if they receive intensive treatment geared to their needs. A team of farsighted physicians, nurses, administrators, social workers and activities therapists demonstrates the fact dramatically in a short-term (average stay, 90 days) mental health unit established several years ago at St. John's Home-Health Care Center in Rochester, N.Y.

Source: Charlotte Isler, RN, *RN* Senior Nursing Editor, "Who Says Senile Geriatric Patients are Untreatable?" *RN*, June 1975.

superstructure without a foundation. To renounce Force and Authority in favor of Fusion and Development creates not a utopia but a failure. To deny the Target Model is to renounce purpose, striving, and the future. To renounce the Established Model is to deny constructive force and useful order in the present.

It is commonly believed that when in a zoo one should do as other specimens do. It is unnecessary, however, for individuals to adopt self-images which correspond to an organization's perception of them. Further, it is unnecessary for self-respect and independence in perception to be achieved at the cost of being judgmental or critical. It is not criticism of organizations that enables an individual to grow; it is understanding and controlled interacting. For individuals to renounce organized activities interrupts their growth as effectively as if organizations had shut them out.

Humans, in their separate beings, are incomplete nonindividuals incapable of surviving infancy, unable to sustain themselves when ill or injured, unable to reproduce, love, share, achieve, exhibit courage, attain respect, or even dispose of their own remains. The Established Model imposes order on such interchangeable nonindividuals. The Target Model at the Fusion level fuses interchangeable units into higher-level units such as marriages, families, and more complex organizations. And Target Model processes at the Development level develop individuality in both the lower and higher units concurrently.

DOMINANCE, TERRITORY, AND ROLES

Dominance

We should not allow our antipathy for the exploitive, self-serving exercise of dominance in zoos and zoo analogues to blind us to the basic importance of dominance in Complete Organizations. In Complete Organizations, dominance maintains needed order, stability, and closure at the level of the Established Model, and needed responsibility, responsiveness, and openness at the level of the Target Model. The mechanism is the same at both levels: enforcing or enabling meaningful roles for individuals. Thus in a herd of grazing animals, sentinels take their places at the periphery of the grazing grounds not according to chance, but according to rank.

When there are disputes within a group of higher animals, the alpha animal invariably intervenes on the side of the lower-ranking member, defending that member's place or role. Even in human organizations there has been a tradition that dominance is not merely a selfish syndrome of might makes right and rank has its privileges. Captains once were the last to leave their ships or would go down with them. But our so-called management sciences were born during this century out of contempt for the masses. Today it is only the nation's president, top officials, and military leaders who will escape inside mountain retreats in the event of atomic war. We hear they will go without their families but take with them their public relations experts.

The United States Constitution was a brilliant consensus on the allocations and denials of governmental functions to governmental units. But our governmental units are now vast operating organizations with their management functions overshadowing their old narrowly defined governmental functions. It may not be important whether any alpha position is filled by election or force. It is obviously important whether or not the position is used to lead the organization up the Hierarchy of Organization Methods or down.

Territory

Robert Ardrey has written a remarkable trilogy of books, *African Genesis, Territorial Imperative*, and *Social Contract*.[4] Given the concepts of territory as he synthesizes them, we can observe with fresh eyes the things we see around us. We can see personal and group territories. We can see that action is at the periphery of a territory, security at the heart. Adventure is outside, boredom within. Stimulation is outside, relaxation within. New ideas are outside, reflection within. Living requires that we alternate, moving in and out.

Territories help us establish our identities. Recognizing this we can observe psychological as well as physical territories. We can learn to carry a territory with us, even on a crowded subway. And we can learn to traverse safely and pleasantly the personal territory of another, perhaps by using no more than a well-timed "Excuse me." Then we can learn to deal with indifference, curiosity, testing, or hostility when we invade a group territory, as when we enter a new school or start a new job.

Familiar surroundings and beings are a basic need. We concentrate our attention by sublimating the familiar and repetitive in an otherwise distracting or overwhelming influx of sensory stimuli. Thus joining a new organization, we may be an unwelcome intrusion and distraction until people become used to us. Obviously, the more novel our appearance and behavior, the longer it may take before we are perceived as familiar and part of the organization.

Role

A lawyer does not invade the territory of an actuary, nor does an accountant invade the territory of a lawyer. Territory in this context clearly is synonymous with responsibility or role. As a generality also, concepts of territory can be expressed as concepts of role. A role provides room for a whole being, permits personal development of skill and performance, and provides a structure for interacting with people and things in the environment. Furthermore, one can have a number of roles in succession or concurrently, such as wife, lawyer, bus passenger, teacher, daughter, mother, friend, customer, et cetera. If dominance is one side of the coin, then territory is the other, and the name of the coin is *role*.

The simplest way to be an ineffectual nonperson is to insist, "I am just me and I don't play roles." So be just you and relate with the same behavior to strangers and friends as to your spouse. Whether driving a car or riding as a passenger, be equally attentive to the road. Expect the same from your students, your children, and your neighbor's children. Be the same in high school, college, and thereafter as you were in elementary school. Cling to unaltering, self-centered behavior, but be aware that identity develops from filling roles, not from denying them.

It has been said that doing things right is less important than doing the right things. In other words, it is less important to master the details of a role than to learn its boundaries. Children demand that parents stay in role. And from my experience in the service fields, more personal failures result from misperception of roles than from inadequacy in performance. Roles are building blocks for organizations and for developing individuality. We need to learn how to select and enter roles, to activate them and deactivate, to reconcile and integrate.

USING ROLES

There is a role for a nurse and there are jobs. There is a role for an accountant and there are jobs. The jobs are of different shapes and levels in thousands of different organizations, and the job descriptions, where they exist, describe job slots and not the roles. Seldom, however, does a job description or a hierarchical superior deny a role. Roles must be relinquished through ignorance, ineptitude, or ambivalence just as they must be achieved through knowledge, skill, and striving.

Work roles evolve from experience, are defined by associations of workers in the same field, and are affirmed by educational institutions (see Figure 8-4). In 1933, my father was president of the New Jersey Society of Certified Public Accountants. He took us with him for dinner one Sunday to meet an economics professor at Rutgers with whom he argued that Rutgers should offer accounting and auditing courses. Today hundreds of colleges offer accounting majors, affirming the role of CPAs. In 1941, a group of company auditors formed an association and pushed for academic courses in what they called *internal auditing* to distinguish it from public accounting. In 1973, the Institute of Internal Auditors, by then numbering approximately 8000 members with chapters in twenty countries, established criteria and examinations for the title Certified Internal Auditor. Today numerous colleges offer courses in internal auditing, confirming the internal auditor's role.

Joining

You join an organization only when you take on a role. In a job you can say nobody told you or the hell with it, but when you take on a role you become part of the whole like a heart in a body or an arm. Thus you make a choice between job and role, selling part of yourself or trying to fulfill, being conditioned by carrot and stick or being an individual. Choose job or role: spouse in a marriage,

FIGURE 8-4

Self-determination of Roles

Who defines the roles of nurses and scientists? Two important examples of how roles are developed.

It is the Association's view that just as questions about the evolving role of the nurse are inevitable so too is conflict in dealing with these questions if the rights of the profession are not recognized. Specifically, determination of the nature and scope of nursing practice is the sole responsibility and obligation of the profession. To deny this right in today's unprecedented period of heightened self-consciousness by individuals and groups is to invite discord. Neither the nursing profession nor its practitioners are willing any longer to participate in professional games and/or relationships whose net effect is to nullify the professional integrity of the nursing practitioner and jeopardize the client's access to effective nursing care services.

This is not to suggest that the profession or its practitioners wish or intend to operate in isolation and apart from other health professions. To do so would be both foolhardy and irresponsible. However, the profession does intend to guard and defend its legitimate professional autonomy. The nursing profession is willing to work in partnership and harmony with the medical profession and the State Education Department in all matters relating to health care. However, the medical profession cannot be the judge of what constitutes nursing practice nor can the State Education Department be a party to or sanction such judgment.

Source: Statement by the New York State Nurses Association, 1974.

*   *   *

The very existence of science depends upon vesting the power to choose between paradigms in the members of a special kind of community. . . .

What are the essential characteristics of these communities? Obviously, they need vastly more study. In this area only the most tentative generalizations are possible. Nevertheless, a number of requisites for membership in a professional scientific group must already be strikingly clear. The scientist must, for example, be concerned to solve problems about the behavior of nature. In addition, though his concern with nature may be global in its extent, the problems on which he works must be problems of detail. More important, the solutions that satisfy him may not be merely personal but must instead be accepted as solutions by many. The group that shares them may not, however, be drawn at random from society as a whole, but is rather the well-defined community of the scientist's professional compeers. One of the strongest, if still unwritten, rules of scientific life is the prohibition of appeals to heads of state or to the populace at large in matters scientific. Recognition of the existence of a uniquely competent professional group and acceptance of its role as the exclusive arbiter of professional achievement has further implications. The group's members, as individuals and by virtue of their shared training and experience, must be seen as the sole possessors of the rules of the game or of some equivalent basis for unequivocal judgments. To doubt that they shared some such basis for evaluations would be to admit the existence of incompatible standards of scientific achievement. That admission would inevitably raise the question whether truth in the sciences can be one.

Source: Thomas S. Kuhn, *Structure of Scientific Revolutions,* The University of Chicago Press, Chicago, 1962, p. 167–168.

parent in a family, nurse or accountant in a service organization, technician, laborer, secretary, customer service representative, hospital patient, student, teacher, food service worker. Jobs are for outsiders, casual, without commitment and externally controlled.

Prerequisite to taking on a role in an organization is a mental picture of patterns of interaction which are mutually satisfactory, beneficial, and responsible. It is the role that must be accepted by the organization, not the individual. Perhaps everyone must start with an organization in a job (apprenticeship, courtship, or whatever as pre-role or junior role) until recognition and development of an appropriate complete role is agreed upon. Acceptance is then by growth into the role. Without roles, an organization is merely a group of individuals, and it is then conventionally held that it is important for them to like each other, to have common backgrounds, tastes, and values, and to have confidence in each other. Thus, without roles, the weaknesses and limitations in understanding of each individual get to be laid on the others, criticizing, putting down, rejecting, and excluding in classic applications of bias and prejudice.

Time utility is a basic economic concept, and joining takes time. To blurt out ideas as soon as one gets them is to deny the utility of timeliness in transactions. To rush things is to regard one's own actions as more important than processes of interaction. To be impatient is to value immediate gratification over development. Impatience and immaturity tend to be linked and to stimulate reactions at the level of Authority instead of acceptance at the level of Fusion.

Participating

Roles place us in a higher unit of organization than our individual selves, and our roles are in a real world, not a symbolic one (see Figure 8-5). Filling a role means that I serve myself and the higher unit concurrently. And it also means that when someone in another role serves that higher unit, I too am served. Six months after my marriage and a year before his death, my father wrote us a letter. The postscript said, "Somehow I can't think of either of you without the two of you—not as separate persons but as a unit of being." He was an organizer.

In my role as a husband I can speak and act for us as a unit or for myself, but not for my wife. She is a separate individual with other roles, such as teacher and nurse in addition to her role as part of us. Likewise my wife for her part can always speak and act for us or for herself, but not for me, because I too am a separate individual with other roles, such as father and comptroller.

To each role I bring my personal identity at its present level and in each role I rise not only by my own efforts but also by the efforts and resistance of others. I gratify and develop myself by gratifying and developing the higher organization. Without a role, I see myself as the center of my world with nothing happening except to me, nothing to be judged except in terms of my pleasure or displeasure, nothing to be understood or learned about others and no way to respond to them except in terms of my feelings.

> The assistant cost accountant had a job, not a role. He explained to me how he prepared a daily scrap report for each factory department using figures that came to him on Form ES132 in the interoffice mail at nine o'clock each morning. Did scrap vary much each day? Not especially. Was his report used in quality control? Probably. Did he know that the Production Control Department also prepared a scrap report? "Why do they do this to me?" Do what? "Make me do all this work when someone else is doing it."

Our roles protect us. If in the office I offer criticism outside my role, then I personally am attacking and I personally can be counterattacked. If I offer advice outside my role, then I become vulnerable to personal judgments about myself and how I fit in as a person. When I stay within my role, all criticism by others, no matter how intended, is converted from an assault on my ego into constructive feedback. If I step out of role, constructive feedback is converted into an assault on my ego. And my role gives me some measure of detachment so I can look at my performance, savor it, evaluate it, and see for myself how to grow in skill and effectiveness. If I do not do these things for myself, I give to others the right and obligation to do them to me.

Participating in roles gives us the Hierarchy of Organization Methods for our personal use. And we become Complete Individuals as we learn to combine in ourselves the Established and the Target Models which together form Complete Organizations

FIGURE 8-5

Living "As If"

Our roles are in a real world, not a symbolic one.

Interacting is a concurrent process, not one person listening today for another who will be talking tomorrow. On the other hand, perhaps the most important of all human innovations in organizing has been the financial concept that actions which are promised or anticipated in the future can be restated and dealt with as if, in fact, they are real actions in the present. Thus, promissory notes are discounted to present values and stocks are bought or sold at prices determined by expectations of future profits. Production plans in the real world of goods and services and personal plans for buying cars or houses get translated into financial projections with feedback and modifications to improve the plans and make them financially feasible.

The sheer power of the financial techniques for moving back and forth in time is fascinating, but the combination of their power and fascination is a growing threat to living productively. To a dangerous extent, manipulation of financial symbols has already become an end in itself. Values have been inverted so that our schools teach and our executives practice management by financial objectives without seeking consensus on objectives and procedures in the real world of goods and services. Financial forecasts assume productivity and exclude the processes of Development in the real world. From these inversions, it has become a logical and widespread practice to hire people and reward them for their potential instead of their performance, for their education and credentials instead of the work they do.

Participating is in the real world and involves us as entire beings. We fill roles and interact with others in their roles by using our present abilities, not our future potentials. When we use plans instead of processes to move into the future, we go only in our minds. Then our planned objectives, severed from our striving, become merely symbolic. We become omnipotent in our disembodied world with solutions for every fantasized problem and with decisions to implement every chosen solution. This is heady stuff indeed, an altered state of consciousness that in small doses has its values. In its addictive stage, however, it means forsaking roles and reality in the present and ripping off real people to maintain the habit.

and higher organisms. But to achieve our individuality, we must be liberated or liberate ourselves to enter the roles to which our processes of living take us, shrinking or expanding the roles to suit our stage and sequence.

Leaving

"Who are you?" was the question in a graduate class at Hunter College. She answered, "Woman, wife, grandmother, nurse, teacher, Republican, sensitive person." Not a practicing nurse or Republican, she kept the roles. Registered as a student, she rejected the student's role because she was learning in the other roles for usefulness in them. Some roles she had left, like child; some roles had been taken from her, like daughter; and some she was reshaping, like mother of grown and married children instead of mother of infants and dependents.

We select jobs or are selected for them in the Established Organizational Model. We accept jobs or are accepted for them in the Target Model. We have roles to develop in the Complete Model, and we develop into them as Complete Individuals. To enter roles and relinquish them is part of the life process. The child who refuses to leave childhood and the great executive who refuses to become an elder statesman are both denying the process, diminishing themselves and the organizations with which they are associated. Writing to us as "one unit of being" after our marriage, my father was not describing us but instead was announcing his recognition of his new role in a changed family organization.

As we mature we accumulate or move through a variety of roles, major and minor, unless we are prevented or prevent ourselves from doing so. Prisoners, oldsters, the unemployed, and other minorities, and women have limited access to many meaningful roles, and their exclusion is to be fought as a disservice both to them and to the organizations and society of which they could be a more meaningful part. On the other hand, individuals may exclude themselves from roles which are available, declining to serve and grow in less than a perfect and hospitable environment and failing to recognize that it is against resistance that they gain their strength. There are no easy roles, easily available, easily filled, and easily relinquished, that are worthwhile.

CONCLUSION

Individuals are part of the continuum of complexification and organization, not apart from it. The same Hierarchy of Organization Methods, therefore, applies to what we call *individuals* and what we call *organizations*. The same organizational models— Established, Target, and Complete—apply to both. And both develop by the same processes at the final level in the Hierarchy of Methods. It is to the processes of Development that we direct our attention in the next chapter.

NOTES

[1] The quotation is one version of a statement attributed to Rabbi Akiba.

[2] Robert Ardrey, *African Genesis,* Atheneum Publishers, New York, 1961, p. 104.

[3] David Cortright, *Soldiers in Revolt: The American Military Today,* Anchor Books, Doubleday & Company, Inc., Garden City, N.Y., 1975.

[4] Robert Ardrey, *African Genesis,* Atheneum Publishers, New York, 1961; *Social Contract,* Dell Publishing Co., Inc., New York, 1974; *Territorial Imperative,* Dell Publishing Co., Inc., New York, 1966.

NINE

Developing and Achieving

It is customary to think of developing as something separate from achieving, to think we should pay for our developing and be paid for our achieving, to think we develop from beginnings but achieve by reaching ends. It is even customary to think of management for ends or by objectives. Developmental psychologists tell us, however, that developing is an active process that includes achieving. And a beginning, as in the case of early farmers moving stones from fields they plowed, can be a coequal objective with an end, like moving stones to a field's perimeter to build a wall. Seeing each end or objective as also a beginning, we can perceive developing and achieving as a single integrated process, simple in concept yet allowing for infinite complexification in application. Teachers and managers alike should nurture the process, not just their timely interests in its beginnings or its ends.

So developing is an active process, but when we are secure and blanketed in the hearts of our territories there is little activity. To develop we must go into the environment, interacting in a cycle or spiral of testing and probing, trying to understand what happens, describing, measuring, classifying, looking for causes, seeking to identify processes, interpreting, clarifying values, and reacting. A more or less conventional set of categories is used here for all the foregoing activities which are subsumed in the spiral of interacting. The categories are (1) testing the environment, (2) making cognitive, and (3) closing the feedback loop.

TESTING THE ENVIRONMENT

During our infancy, parents provide us with secure territories and smooth our interacting with the environment outside. During childhood we start to venture forth alone, but if we go without errands or seeking roles and without their directions and objectives, then we go as spectators instead of participants and we can interact only by staring and being amused or dismayed. As spectators our signs read, "Push me aside if I'm in the way," and we cannot gain regard or self-esteem. Going out to run errands or fill roles, we perceive them to be obstructed before we ourselves can be. It is satisfying to carry through on errands despite "snow or rain or gloom of night"[1] and to defend our roles, because good feelings arise from what we do instead of bad feelings from what fate or others do or say against us. Within roles we develop as complete, well-organized individuals by interacting at all levels in the Hierarchy of Organization Methods.

Auditing in the Established and Target Models

The financial records of a business are supposed to run parallel to actual operations, but occasionally they diverge. To test the validity of records and bring them back in line when necessary, auditors compare records with reality in two principal ways: inventories are counted and matched with balances on the books and customers are asked to confirm that they owe what the records show. I once visited a great open-pit copper mine in the Southwest and spent a couple of days in its supply warehouses seeing how they kept records and how they received, stored, issued, and counted the supplies. In remote regions spare parts and operating supplies are hard to come by and top management at the mine had stressed their control since the days of mule trains. Millions of dollars of goods were there and dozens of people worked at physical handling and at keeping the records of receipts, requisitions, and balances, item by item.

Testing gave superlative results. Discrepancies between physical counts and book records had always been statistically insignificant. There was compliance with authority, stated objectives were being met, prescribed procedures were being followed, stock was well cared for, and the records were neat and accurate. But tests within the Established Organizational Model tell us only about the Established Model. To the time of my visit, questions had not been asked or tests applied to disclose the fantastically low productivity of the supply warehousing, its inversion of procedure and purpose which is commonplace in the Established Model, its engendering of large economic losses, and its horrible wasting of human potentials. Evidence of all these things remained invisible over the years, sublimated of necessity by those who wished to work there and outside the perception models of any observers who could communicate their findings.

Inventories were taken monthly as well as at year-end. Throughout the year, shortages in counts were disposed of by preparing special requisitions which were given arbitrary cost center designations and which were processed as if genuine. Overages in counts were disposed of by moving the excess items to a "surplus" area in the warehouse. The system operated perfectly to conceal losses or thefts, to conceal knowledge of "surplus" stock for any legitimate purpose, and to destroy the integrity of the cost records. Furthermore, over one-third of the items in inventory had unit values of less than 25 cents. Over one-third of the requisitions were for less than $1, and some were for pennies— such as "one pearl eraser, item OS2183," which was requisitioned by the accounting office and priced at 4 cents, or "three steel washers, one inch diameter, item RG8175," requisitioned by the truck repair garage and priced at 8 cents. There were no supply cabinets in the office or parts bins in the garage. From the moment a mechanic found need for a part until a requisition could be prepared, approved, sent to the warehouse, filled, and the part delivered, the elapsed time was at least one hour. Instead of assuring that supplies were quickly available when and where needed, the system operated perfectly and at great cost to make sure of the opposite.

Measuring in the Established and Target Models

In the Established Model we lay our measurements on people, using normal distributions to rank them, comparisons with standards to fail and reject them, and negative exponential curves to distribute the loot. In the Target Model we lay our measurements on organizations as described in Chapter 3. Our models and our methods are coordinate, so we enforce the status quo by supervision but enforce progress by review. In the Complete Model, where Authority enforces the process of developing, we can perceive and measure progress as the inverse of clarity; the blurring of the boundaries as in a snapshot shows us the direction and extent of movement.

How should an urban school system adjust to the urban financial crisis? In an editorial on July 25, 1975,[2] *The New York Times* addressed itself to this issue with clarity in terms of the Established Perception Model:

> Resort to larger classes is . . . the wrong and unacceptable response to the crisis. Fortunately, it is also an unnecessary measure, readily avoidable if the system insists instead on new yardsticks of productivity and efficiency. . . . For example, the most recent assessment by a group of education and management experts confirms that the existing system of so-called preparation periods for teachers could readily be curtailed without resulting in personal or professional hardship. . . . Nor does it seem unreasonable to ask teachers, whose normal school day at present runs to six hours and twenty minutes, to extend their daily working time by thirty or forty minutes. . . . Redundant administrative positions must be abolished and supervisors should be required to take a more active part in classroom teaching. . . . Students can contribute to easing the budget squeeze by giving up excessively liberal privileges of free school transportation.

Making teachers and administrators do a little more for a little less and taking back transportation tokens from students ties down the safety valves to meet a crisis. Our crucial need is to change directions, moving up the Hierarchy of Methods instead of down, and adding a Target Model to our schools. Too little consensus exists on either methods or objectives in urban schools, if we judge by continuous fighting for control between professionals, parents, politicians, and the courts. Too few students have taken on their essential roles as producers in what should be a learning-teaching system, if we judge by truancy rates and disciplinary problems. Reaching for more efficiency and rejecting in the Established Model without concurrent reaching for more consensus and accepting in the Target Model means regressing and pulling down. Achieving is part of the process of developing, not regressing.

Figure 9-1 analyzes a teacher's day in school in minutes. The *Times* editorial calls for eliminating the preparation period, leaving no time for teachers to preview audio-visual material, no time for meetings with individual students or parents, no time for anything but routine work. Efficiency can be gained by shunting aside all special thought or individual responses, but I know of no evidence that this can improve productivity in a service organization. To the contrary, one can find impressive testimony in the recollections of successful adults to the importance during their school years of some personal one-on-one contact with a teacher.

There can be some utility in looking at a teacher's day in school and measuring effectiveness as the product of three factors: (1) percentage of time in school spent working, (2) percentage of working time spent teaching, and (3) percentage of teaching time spent teaching effectively. For the first factor, we should expect no more than the 80 percent standard used in factories and on construction jobs—teachers no less than hospital, office, and other workers need cleanup time, toilet time, and coffee breaks. The teacher in our case study meets the standard, even if we make the horrendous assumption that time spent monitoring in corridors and study halls is not to be counted as working time.

Factor two highlights an important organizational problem—building a record takes precedence over work. Using teachers as clerks makes school administrators look good, because it builds records with apparent efficiency and the loss in teaching time is not easily seen or measured. According to our case study in Figure 9-1, clerical work and chores take 32 percent of the teacher's total time in school. In terms of so-called working time, clerical work and chores are 40 percent and classroom teaching 50 percent.

> Recognition of failure dawns slowly in a bureaucracy, but dawned it has in California prison treatment circles. Prison psychiatrists who are willing to level with reporters admit they now spend 90% of their time on paperwork, writing up reports based on perfunctory annual interviews with prisoners.[3]

FIGURE 9-1

Case Study of a Teacher's Day in School in Minutes

(This does not include preparation, grading, etc., outside school.)

	Total minutes	Lunch	Monitoring	Clerical work	Preparation period	Teaching
8:55- 9:00	5			5		
9:00- 9:15	15			15		
9:15- 9:18	3		3			
9:18- 9:58	40			10		30
9:58-10:01	3		3			
10:01-10:41	40			10		30
10:41-10:44	3		3			
10:44-11:24	40			10		30
11:24-11:27	3		3			
11:27-12:07	40	30		10		
12:07-12:10	3		3			
12:10-12:50	40			10	30	
12:50-12:53	3		3			
12:53- 1:33	40		25	15		
1:33- 1:36	3		3			
1:36- 2:16	40			10		30
2:16- 2:19	3		3			
2:19- 2:59	40			10		30
2:59- 3:10	11			11		
Total school time	375	30	49	116	30	150
% of total time	100	8	13	31	8	40
% of "working" time				40	10	50

Other examples come readily to mind, such as doctors ordering tests just for the record because of the dangers of malpractice suits. People in organizations see dangers too and build protective records. This is a problem to be confronted if we are to improve the productivity of organizations.

Factor three is the percentage of classroom teaching time spent teaching effectively. Unless the system has enlisted students as producers, a high rating could be 25 percent and we assume that here. Multiplying the rating of each of the three factors, $.80 \times .50 \times .25$, we arrive at an effectiveness score of 10 percent. In other words, out of a school day of 375 minutes, only one-quarter of the classroom minutes, or $37\frac{1}{2}$ minutes, are rated as effective. If we shift the preparation period to classroom teaching, on the experts presumption that preparation periods are useless, we increase effectiveness only to 12 percent, calculated as $.80 \times .60 \times .25$. Productivity cannot be improved if problems of organization and work are unseen or treated as if they were people problems.

Testing Is Appreciating

We test our environment not to judge it but to make it known. If we fear the unknown in our environment, by testing we can make it known and appreciate it. In *The New York Times* for May 4, 1975, Kent Garland Burtt describes the Early Learning Center in Stamford, Connecticut:

> Teachers seldom ask questions like "What's that shape called?" or "How many beads are in the jar?" Such testing is seen as causing an unnecessary twinge of fear. They can tell what the child knows by how he works with materials, matching, counting or filling in missing parts of a matrix. . . . Mrs. Skutch will invite or offer, but won't cajole or manipulate. If a child doesn't want to produce or participate, he can watch, wander and absorb, thereby testing the value of an activity.

MAKING COGNITIVE

Much learning apparently takes place outside the realm of conscious cognition and, therefore, outside the scope of control by Authority. We cannot order ourselves to learn to walk or talk, and we cannot supervise such complex learning in ourselves or others. We can, however, consciously start the process of learning and developing and persist in it. Two ways to enforce and reinforce the process of learning, developing, and achieving are discussed in this section.

Making Policies Instead of Decisions

Policies can be formed only by thinking, but decisions can be made by the flip of a coin. Policies define a process and include a purpose. Decisions, orders, rules, and regulations define what to do and how to do it, but exclude both process and purpose. Policies assign responsibility to those who do the work; decisions sever responsibility from work and substitute compliance. Dominance and decisiveness unchecked by Fusion cause regression, as in the condition called amblyopia where a subordinated eye becomes blurred or blind.

> "In making decisions on employee benefits," the executive of a small business observed, "I am constantly torn between being humane and doing my job of making profits for the company. For example, our purchasing director had a stroke twelve weeks ago and may be out as many more. Each month so far I decided to continue full salary, but how can I justify those decisions and when must I stop?"

The answer, of course, is making a policy instead of decisions. Disability pay is compensation, not charity, and it can be provided through standard insurance contracts. For all employees the benefit is the protection provided, and the level of that protection, like the level of compensation in every form, is subject to analysis and negotiation. If decisions are made, they tend to become precedents to be copied in the future without consideration of the reasons for them, like length of service in some disability payment plans.

When Authority at the top is used to make decisions, the regressive process continues until no action is volunteered; no studying is done or work performed except as decided and ordered by the teacher or work supervisor. When Authority at the top is used to form policies, it forces decision making and responsibility on students and workers, giving them roles and reinforcing their processes of development.

Teachers and supervisors tend to be strict and bossy or weak and indecisive, according to our perception models. Political leaders and teenagers on the streets personalize problems in terms of their own credibility and see attempts to reach consensus as a weakening of their authority. Decisive actions are then taken to assert machismo, like sending in marines and fighting in the streets. For most problems in the world there is no single answer or solution, of course, but only an approach or process of developing and achieving. Nonetheless, leaders tend to see themselves required to make decisions instead of to enforce the process. Students and employees with vested interests in the rules and regulations of the establishment maintain their positions by pushing decision making up the hierarchy. Skilled bureaucrats protect themselves by seeking written directives for everything they do.

Despite decision-avoiding subordinates, a boss can enforce the process of developing and achieving without appearing weak or indecisive.

> Early on as comptroller of The Rockefeller Foundation, I found the number of documents requiring the comptroller's signature appalling. One day three copies of a budget revision were handed to me for signing and other things were on my mind. "Is this right? Good, but you initial them before I sign." The staff person declined and asked to take them back for further checking. A policy was announced that initials of the person responsible for the work must always be affixed before asking for the comptroller's signature. Enforcing the policy helped the department to start organizing itself by responsibility instead of authority.

Despite decision-making bosses in Established Model organizations, individual students and employees can own their personal processes of developing and achieving:

1. In general, subordinates select and define for their superiors the decisions to be made. One middle manager used to take the most annoying, petty, and irresponsible

questions of his subordinates to his superior. The superior was delighted to have so many easy decisions to make and thus, happily preoccupied, did not interfere on important matters or appear to be aware of them.

2. When superiors avoid making policies, subordinates can make them. The editor of a column in an educational magazine was frustrated by a vice-president who deleted at least one item from every column because it "didn't seem to fit." The editor wrote a policy statement with criteria for selecting column items and sent it to the vice-president. No items were deleted thereafter.

3. Lack of responsiveness can be turned to advantage. A middle manager was dismayed that annual reports for her department elicited no response from her superiors. Then she started inserting statements of new departmental policies and plans in each report. The lack of response became her authorization to proceed.

Reviewing and Summarizing

In general, people equate work with handling details in the present tense; working hard is thought to mean getting out a lot of work, like answering a lot of questions. When a teacher answers a student's question in class, he is working. After a class when he recalls and reconsiders all the questions by all the students he appears not to be working, but his effort may result in identifying a common pattern or cause for a group of questions. In a future class he may then be able to deal directly with the basic cause, once and for all eliminating numerous questions which would have required individual answers.

Reviewing and summarizing is uncomfortable work. It is self-imposed and easy to avoid; bits and pieces of "real work" always seem to take precedence. It is hard to measure and its value has to be demonstrated repeatedly before it is accepted by either workers or administrators as an organizational necessity. On the other hand, we find consultants and management trainees who contact a work situation only by means of reviewing and summarizing. Their perspective, insights, and work-saving recommendations are too often attributed to their personal brilliance and technical background instead of the methodology they use.

What is the methodology? The first step in summarizing is to establish categories. In simple sorting, two commonly used categories are item type and size. The items can also be sorted in terms of the kind and extent of work to be performed on them. A frequency distribution by one of the preceding categories against a time scale is often significant.

The second step is to maintain records. Patterns and trends are obscured by short-term fluctuations unless counts and measurements are made and records maintained. A 5 percent change in annual workload is seldom apparent to the buyer in the purchasing office, the nurse in the emergency room, or the voucher typist in an accounting office. If reductions in workload are not noticed, Parkinson's law states that the available work will expand to fill the available time of the buyer, nurse, or voucher typist.

The third step is to experiment to see if significant patterns can be developed. For example, a fire department might expect to find variations in the incidence of false alarms: perhaps more in the summer than the winter, more in the afternoon than the morning. Significant variations in types of fires and geographical areas involved could also be anticipated, such as a peak in residential fires during a spell of cold weather.

The simplest method of review is a film of some action which can be replayed and re-viewed. This method is used both in sports and in time-and-motion studies. Musicians use recordings to re-hear their work as a basis for adjustment and improvement. Writers re-read and re-write. Systems of internal control are most effective when they stress review and proofs in total instead of detailed checking as the work progresses. Auditing has moved beyond financial records to operational reviews and performance audits. The Hospital Utilization Review Boards required under Medicare are examples of the increasing recognition given to the importance of review in all fields.

In any organization where reviewing and summarizing are not carried out and used on a continuing basis, Pareto's law will apply: 20 percent of the work will produce 80 percent of the results; the remaining 80 percent of the work will produce only 20 percent of the results. In other words the remaining 80 percent of the work will be only one-sixteenth as productive as the first 20 percent. Startling as this may seem, it is probably an understatement, not an exaggeration, in the average situation.

Example 1. Thirty-seven percent of the orders placed by a purchasing department were found to be for personal orders for officers and overseas staff.

Example 2. A billing department of six clerks never worked overtime. Over a five-year period the number of bills prepared in the peak month of each year was five times the lowest month and twice the next highest.

Example 3. "At least one-third of all arrests in the United States are for public drunkenness. In some cities the proportion runs as high as three-fourths. The commitment of police on the street and for processing at the station house, the commitment of time by judges, court administrators and courtrooms—all this constitutes an enormous drain on a justice system that is already overtaxed by felony cases. This misuse of tax supported resources is bad enough, and constitutes a problem crying out for solution. But still more important is the fact that this system is absolutely ineffective as a deterrent."[4]

CLOSING THE FEEDBACK LOOP

Some years ago on an August day, I stood outside the Canyon Village cafeteria in Yellowstone Park with my twelve-year-old daughter. An aluminum door to the plaza had been open, and we watched an employee start to close it. It failed to latch. He banged it again without success, then several times more in rapid sequence. When he paused, my daughter noticed a small stone by the door sill, but the worker had eyes only for the latch. He put his shoulder to the door, forced it and bent it, then shifted his gaze to the level of the stone which had caused the problem.

A problem in the past can be solved, in the present can be avoided, and in the future can be prevented. By changing their focus, individuals and organizations change the problems they perceive and their methods of solution. The perception of a problem can be self-centered, in which case the solution is to avoid criticism; centered on short-run objectives, in which case the solution is to be expedient; or centered on organization and work, in which case the solution is to enforce the process of developing and achieving. Feedback in its simplest form is a straight rebound like an echo or a reflection in a mirror. More useful, however, is complex feedback which changes the problems or which processes the data and returns them in different forms. Closing the loop so feedback is received, whether from self-review or from outside, is essential for developing and achieving in individuals and organizations.

In mathematical analysis, the classic example of a simple control system is the furnace-thermostat loop. The thermostat receives and processes data on temperature and compares the data with the thermostat setting or goal. When the temperature falls below the setting, a message is sent that turns the furnace on. When the temperature rises above the setting, a message is sent that turns the furnace off. If the loop is broken, the system goes off on a tangent. Organizations and individuals go off on tangents too if they lack a feedback loop or it is broken. Three concepts involved in closing the loop and keeping it closed are discussed in the remaining sections of this chapter. They are (1) setting priorities, (2) rejecting or shifting work, and (3) assigning responsibility.

Setting Priorities

Target Model Organizations are always confronted with more work than they can accomplish. There is always more health care to be delivered and more instruction to be given. There are always more roads to be repaired, more streets to be cleaned, and more fires to be prevented. Setting priorities must be a continuing process.

When nurses go on duty in a hospital, they first ascertain the status of patients in their areas. The critically ill must have first call on their attention and emergencies first call on their services. Giving medications and infusions, suctioning mucus, responding to questions, preparing for operations, counseling relatives, checking diets, helping doctors, observing conditions—these, among other duties, constitute more work than can be done completely on one shift. Judgment must be exercised in defining priorities, and with experience and education nurses define them better and move through them more rapidly and effectively. Nursing care is a purposeful process, and nurses can grow in their role for many years.

All too often organizations take away from employees the responsibility for defining priorities. With their work prescribed for them, employees then focus on how to make their jobs easier. Education is often structured in a system that defines limited areas of concern and fixed standards within those areas. The content of statewide examinations may control the content of a course. Then a course outline cuts the content into segments of fixed dimensions. Confined within this structure, teachers year by year accumulate notes, tests, and lesson plans which not only make their jobs progressively easier, but also give them a vested interest in maintaining the status quo.

Dividing work into neat segments which can be completed deprives the worker of responsibility for growing and improving. It is impossible to conceive that in a hospital the work of a nurse's aide, practical nurse, registered nurse, intern, or attending physician can ever be done except in terms of some arbitrary assignment of work. Only if responsibility for selecting priorities is part of every job can there be continuing growth in skill and productivity. The misconception that systems and procedures must define limits of work results in breaking the feedback loop, preventing change, and automatically freezing or reducing productivity.

Rejecting or Shifting Work

The obverse to setting priorities is rejecting work or shifting it to others. Don't expect to find this responsibility set forth in many job descriptions. In its absence, however, jobs are defined in terms of rote (here is what to do), bowing to authority (do whatever you are told), conditioned reflexes (take care of whatever is put on your desk or whoever walks through the door), or simply being helpful.

The thought of being helpful is tremendously seductive. In administering company fringe benefits, the benefits administrator who offers to help employees in filing their medical claims by soliciting questions, calling the insurance company, and relaying answers, finds gratification in being helpful but reduces the job to that of a nonproductive go-between. When called to task because important work is undone, the administrator gives a standard hurt response, "I was only trying to be helpful; isn't that what I am supposed to do?" The hurt is probably justified in terms of complaints, criticism, and occasional praise received in the past.

Getting in the middle is the ultimate political goal under a hierarchical system of organization, because it is the most secure position of prestige and power. The president, located between the board of directors and the organization, controls the flow of information to the board and relays back its policies, authorizations, and feelings, both expressed and surmised. Officers and secretaries become established around the president, relaying information back and forth to others who then must bow to authority and do what they are told. The go-between role can provide relative freedom from responsibility and relief from pressure for personal productivity. Almost inevitably, however, the person in the middle breaks the closed loop of doing, reviewing, and adapting, of testing the environment, making cognitive, and feeding back.

Assigning Responsibility

Whenever authority or control is exercised over someone, that person is relieved of responsibility. Just as authority flows down through the go-between, so does responsibility flow up through that person. Only at the bottom of the line, at the most detailed level of work, are the consequences apparent. At this point we can observe a clerk spending two days preparing a $5 refund claim or a pharmacist preparing individually labeled daily prescriptions for 500 patients in a methadone maintenance clinic.

Relieved of responsibility, a worker has no alternative to following orders. Deprived of a closed loop, the worker must rely on precedent instead of purpose. The job then becomes taking care of whatever is put on the desk and whoever walks through the door. At higher organizational levels a technique for shunting executives aside is to load their desks with trivia. If work is never rejected, much or most of it becomes nonproductive or unimportant. If work is never shifted to someone else, much or most of it becomes a duplicated effort which someone else has already done or is set up to do.

Of course, work cannot be shifted unless there is knowledge of what other workers do and who the work belongs to. Imagine a football team if each player knows only what he is supposed to do and has no idea of the roles of teammates. Imagine further that he is not informed as to the purpose of any play, not even whether it is a pass or run. Then he is in the position of the average office worker. If he knows the purpose and is unable to adjust his activities to achieve it, he is in the position of the typical student or teacher. In fact, any assertion of independent, personal responsibility on the part of a student, teacher, hospital patient, or office worker is obviously disruptive of the normal routine, nonconforming and disturbing in the Established Organizational Model.

Work is as important as play and potentially as enjoyable. Work should be organized in a closed loop of purpose, coordinated effort, review, and modification. Assigning responsibility is more important than establishing lines of authority if the objective is to achieve high productivity. Responsibility closes the loop; authority opens it.

PERCEPTION AND MEASUREMENT

It has been estimated by a leading engineering college that the half-life of a technical education is eight years. In other words, half of what is learned will be irrelevant or obsolete eight years later. This may be a reasonable approximation, but even allowing for substantial error, it has many implications as to productivity. To begin with, an equivalent statement in terms of work is that the nature of technical work changes at the rate of 8.3 percent a year compounded annually. It follows that continuing education must be associated with such work. In this context, nurses, tax accountants, and teachers are among those for whom developing must be a continuous process if they are to work effectively.

The rate of change in technical work can be split into two parts. First is the rate at which the relevance or usefulness of acquired knowledge and skills is affected by environmental changes which reduce demand for them. Second is the rate at which knowledge and skills must be upgraded by new knowledge and advanced skills for doing the same work. Books like *Age of Discontinuity*[5] and *Future Shock*[6] confirm our personal observations of rapid changes in the environment which impact on all work at all levels. Voucher typists in their relatively low-skill jobs are seen to have no need or way to upgrade their skills, so they are simply displaced when computers take over voucher preparation. An equally valid perception, however, is to include voucher typists among those for whom developing must be a continuous process. Instead of being rejected and discarded, voucher typists can become keypunch operators, coders, stenographers, or whatever else is next in line in their organization. In this sense then, voucher typists, file clerks, and nurses' aides are also among those who do work in which developing must be a continuing process.

Nursing, tax accounting, and teaching can be structured in either roles or jobs, and the productivity of the organization will rise or fall accordingly. Voucher typing, filing, and assisting can be structured in roles consisting of interconnected job clusters or in jobs which are dead-end, and the productivity of the organization will rise or fall accordingly. When a major survey asks top managers how the productivity of their organizations can be improved and top managers respond that their decision making and control is the major factor, we see their contempt for developing and achieving by anyone but themselves.[7] And we see something about what schools of business are teaching as they perform their function of confirming the dominion which managers assert.

CONCLUSION

The processes of Developing were presented in this chapter and those of Fusion and Authority in earlier chapters. Processes of Force and Influence have been touched upon in this book only to the extent required to meet their purposes. Now we can invert the Hierarchy of Methods to show Developing as its foundation, beginning with the crying and striving of an infant, progressing to purposeful calling and striving toward a symbiotic relationship with a parent at the Fusion level. Then socialization at the Influence level occurs, to smooth the way to a broader range of interrelationships in which order is maintained by Authority and backed by Force. Integrity, culture, values, purpose, mutuality, and development are not superimposed on Force and Authority; they come first, and Force and Authority are meaningless and incompetent except in their support.

What remains is to discuss in Chapter 10 the operating of a Complete Organization and in Chapter 11 some extended and comprehensive examples. Then in Chapter 12 we must face up to the question of why we should strive for more productivity and more individual achievement in a world that already has more of them than top managers can manage.

NOTES

[1] "Snow or rain or gloom of night" is a slightly corrupted extract of the inscription on a New York City post office.

[2] *New York Times,* July 25, 1975. The complete text of the editorial follows:

Shanker's Fear Tactics

Albert Shanker has now stooped to aping the "fear city" scare tactics of the police union. In predicting that the austerity budget will leave classrooms too crowded for learning and the schools abandoned to violence, the president of the United Federation of Teachers is trying to persuade parents that their children can be saved from chaos only by surrender to his union's excessive demands.

Mr. Shanker has compounded his dismal rhetoric by asking for teachers' pay raises "in excess of 20 percent." Even if discounted as the usual hyperbole accompanying contract negotiations, these demands are clearly inflammatory at a time when a wage freeze is widely considered the only means of averting disaster for the city as well as for the municipal work force itself.

Such deliberate distortions ought not to deceive the public about the actual options open to the Board of Education in adjusting its $2.7-billion budget to the grim fiscal realities without abandoning educational quality. Resort to larger classes is, as we have consistently maintained as adamantly as Mr. Shanker, the wrong and unacceptable response to the crisis. Fortunately, it is also an unnecessary measure, readily avoidable if the system insists instead on new yardsticks of productivity and efficiency. The many wasteful practices which have been sanctified by contract and custom can and must be eliminated.

The sacrifices to be asked of teachers amount to little more than the discontinuation of luxuries in staffing which should never have been approved and which the city can no longer afford. For example, the most recent assessment by a group of education and management experts confirms that the existing system of so-called preparation periods for teachers could readily be curtailed without resulting in personal or professional hardship. Such a step would allow the maintenance of present class size—or even its desirable further reduction—with a smaller teaching force at considerable savings.

Nor does it seem unreasonable to ask teachers, whose normal school day at present runs to six hours and twenty minutes, to extend their daily working time by thirty or forty minutes. While such action would obviously be in the pupils' interest, it should not be overlooked that teachers also benefit directly from manageable class size. Indeed, the teachers' burden could be further lightened by more effective use of selected and trained volunteers.

Redundant administrative positions must be abolished and supervisors should be required to take a more active part in classroom teaching. Decentralized community school districts need to be held strictly accountable in their fiscal operations. The counterproductive practice of allowing the Board of Education's lay members to maintain costly executive assistants and other personal staffs should be stopped.

Students can contribute to easing the budget squeeze, by giving up excessively liberal privileges of free school transportation. Maintenance costs could probably be reduced significantly if students shared in the work of keeping the schools clean. Wasteful practices and a myriad of expensive privileges, such as excessive sabbaticals and sick leaves and lax teacher attendance rules, have inflated the schools' budgets.

It is simply not true, as Mr. Shanker threatens, that an austerity budget is incompatible with sound educational quality. But there is clearly disaster at the end of the line if expenditures are to remain frozen at levels dictated by union truculence, administrative rigidity and a business-as-usual mentality in the face of the present emergency.

[3] Jessica Mitford, *Kind and Usual Punishment,* Alfred A. Knopf, Inc., New York, 1973.

[4] Ramsey Clark, *Crime in America,* Pocket Books, Inc., New York, 1970.

[5] Peter Drucker, *Age of Discontinuity,* Harper & Row, Publishers, Incorporated, New York, 1969.

[6] Alvin Toffler, *Future Shock,* Random House, Inc., New York, 1971.

[7] Herman S. Jacobs, with Katherine Jillson, *Executive Productivity,* American Management Association, New York, 1974. There are numerous references in this survey report to the idea that management controls all organizational productivity. For example, there are these two sentences on page 13: "Apparently, it is increasingly being recognized that productivity in general is firmly linked to executive productivity. In a sense, the managers and presidents in the survey are taking productivity responsibility upon their shoulders." Remember that this is what managers and presidents say about themselves.

TEN

Developing and Maintaining the Complete Organization

Systems analysis is not expected to provide useful information about matters outside the system being analyzed. Reactions of those in the Established Model to its processes should not be expected to provide useful information about processes in the Target Model. In the Established Model the masses may see Force and Authority as holding them down and restricting them, with the only apparent alternative being freedom. Management, on the other hand, tends to see Force and Authority as necessary for law, order, and efficiency, with the only apparent alternative being chaos and inefficiency. There is nothing viable about having no organization at all, no organizational structure, no processes, and no responsibilities. Such nullities are not features of the Target Model and Complete Organization described in this book. Tearing down is not the same as building up. Adding a Target Model is not the same as destroying the Established one.

In the musical *The King and I*, Anna added a Target Model to the king's Established Model, thereby achieving a Complete Service Organization. Force can get boats rowed or cotton picked, but Force alone cannot educate. Fusion is required between teaching and learning if there is to be education and development. Authority can get machines used efficiently to produce material goods and store and deliver them in accordance with market demands, but it cannot produce and store services for future delivery. There must be step-by-step coordination between those who need services and the organizations which respond to their needs. It is not optional whether or not there is a Target Model in service organizations—services simply cannot be produced effectively in the Established Model.

It is possible to create an Established Model Organization on paper, but a Complete Organization must grow, develop, and mature, whether the organization is a single person, a couple, family, school, hospital, or other multiperson organization. In this chapter we are concerned with how Complete Organizations can be developed and maintained. In many cases, this means starting with an Established Model, adding a Target Model, and controlling the ebb and flow between the two.

CONTROLLING PASSAGE AND ADMISSIONS

The Complete Organization can be visualized as having the shape of an hourglass with an inside ladder connecting the two parts. Jobs are in the lower part, which symbolizes the Established Model, and roles are in the upper part, which symbolizes the Target Model. The boss is stationed at the passage between the two parts and controls any movement between them. The boss can pass people up the ladder to the Target Model to a position overhead, can pull people down to the Established Model under foot, or can destroy the ladder.

The boss also controls admission to the organization. In the Established Model of schools, hospitals, and other service organizations, there are no organizational slots for students, patients, and other receivers of services, so admitting them merely means they are eligible to be dispensed to, treated, or otherwise administered to by the organization. In the Target Model of service organizations, on the other hand, there are responsible organizational roles for students and patients and in the Target Model the boss negotiates and enforces contracts between the organization and its members, including those the organization serves.

Career Ladders

In the Established Model, the Peter principle[1] states that workers are promoted until they reach their levels of incompetency. Even a casual observer can see that the principle has considerable validity, and the validity can be explained. Good performance in one job slot is rarely a guide to good performance in another, because job slots use only parts of people and each promotion calls for a somewhat different part. In fact good performance on the job is often a contraindication to promotion because it indicates a worker has been properly placed. So instead of being based on performance, promotions in the Established Model are commonly based on tests or estimates of aptitude or potential. These too have limited predictive value, because success in filling a new job slot is as much a matter of compliances, submissions, covering of flanks, and refraining from doing certain things as it is of doing certain other things efficiently. No wonder, then, that bosses in the Established Model say that the productivity of their organizations is mostly a matter of their own personal expertise and wise business decisions.

As to the Target Model, first the good news: workers develop within their roles, extending the roles to the limits of their competencies and then perhaps stepping into new roles. Now the bad news: the Target Model is no bed of roses, no nursery filled with gentle sweetness, no utopia where the terrors of responsibility and the hassles of life are blocked out. To the contrary. It is not in the Target Model, but only in the job slots of the Established Model, that workers can retreat from living.

So how do we convert jobs into roles? First, we make learning a part of every job. In the Established Model the higher-ups are paid to learn (e.g., professors to do research, systems analysts to study specifications of new equipment, managers to attend seminars), but workers are paid only to work. If we mix learning with producing, however, we distort or lose our measurements of output per working hour, which is a basic control in the Established Model. Only a fool discards a control without having a substitute on hand; therefore, introducing learning into every job requires the simultaneous introduction of a new control.

Essentially the new control is to pair the opportunity with the problem, the gain with the cost. The voucher typist is told, "If you want to study shorthand, we will schedule training sessions for an hour each day, half during working hours and half after, but you have to get all your regular work done anyway." The payroll supervisor is told, "You seem interested in taxes. Look over the tax services and tax magazines in some college library and decide which ones we should have here. Then rearrange the work in your section so you can spend one-third of your time reading taxes. But all payroll work has to get done, remember that." The data processing room personnel are told, "Instead of working five days of seven hours each week, you can work four days of eight and three-quarters hours. But the data processing room is to be open and the computer running all five days. That means only half of you will be here on some days and at least two or three of you must know every job. Tell me if you want to try the new schedule and when you can fully meet the requirements that go with it."

People are now passing into the Target Model, some of them only part-time or partway, a few completely with a great rush and release of abilities, a few not at all. There will be recalls to mobilize for sudden rush jobs, and there will be regressions under stress. But roles in the Target Model are being established. And oddly enough, investing in the future may even be paying off in the present, with output per working hour going up instead of down.

Personal Adjustments

Moving from the Established Model to a Complete Organization is tough on the boss. Instead of just having underlings to look down on, evaluate, direct, and motivate, the boss also has staff overhead to look up to and they are not only telling the boss about new unknown problems but are giving solutions too. By getting involved too much or in the wrong way, the boss then intrudes into staff roles, thereby destroying responsibility and pushing the staff down again into subordinate jobs in the Established Model.

What is a boss supposed to do in the Target Model? The boss is supposed to coordinate, to help the team recognize all aspects of problems and solutions, and to enlist the efforts of all staff members in relevant roles. The boss is also a principal instrument for testing the environment outside the unit and returning with useful feedback. In addition, the boss plays a leading role in deciding what future adjustments are called for as a result of failures or mistakes. If staff members drop off the team by covering up mistakes or by failing to learn from them, the boss must make their departure official.

What is a boss supposed to do in a Complete Organization? Theodore Roosevelt said to speak softly but carry a big stick. It is more complicated than that. The boss must know roles in both the Target and the Established Models, where the staff is, and how to control their passage between the two models. The boss must use or oppose societal Influence which also affects the movement of staff. When the organization develops to a reasonable balance between the two models, the boss must find a supplementary work role, because being boss will no longer be a full-time activity.

It should also be noted that each staff member who moves up from a job slot in the Established Model to a role in the Target Model has major personal adjustments to make. In job slots workers are precluded from knowing what others do, but in roles they must relate to the roles of others and must understand organizational objectives. It is not increased technical competence alone that moves people up into the Target Model and earns them places on the team.

Admissions

Admitting consumers as partners in production helps service organizations to be responsive, but there can be too much undiluted responsiveness. Most activities must be carried on routinely. Multiperson organizations must use consciousness as carefully as individuals do. Standard operating procedures are equivalent in a multiperson organization to habits in an individual person; only as standard procedures become progressively more superimposed and interrelated in the Established Model can the organization become progressively more responsive to higher levels of challenge and satisfaction in the Target Model.

It follows that jobs and roles for students, patients, and other consumers of services must be carefully delineated in advance. The admission process should clarify rights, obligations, and expectations. If consumers are to be treated as copartners, they must earn their roles by learning, among other things, to understand, respect, and relate to the roles of others. In long-lasting roles such as that of student, people should demonstrate increasing responsibility, because developing and achieving go hand in hand with the organizational role of consuming and producing. Furthermore, consumers as coproducers must tolerate and adapt to the plateaus and regressions in the growth and development of the organization to at least the same extent as the organization must tolerate and adapt to the inevitable plateaus and regressions of its members in their roles.

The admissions procedure should be contractual on both sides, not selective and judgmental. The office of admissions in service organizations should be renamed the *office of admission contracts*.

Productivity

Productivity means efficiency in the Established Model and effectiveness in the Target Model. For manufacturers of physical goods, effectiveness is assumed to be controlled in the competitive marketplace where goods sell only if they are effective in meeting consumer preferences, needs, and demands. For service organizations, however, effectiveness is not controllable in the marketplace, and there are a number of reasons why this is so.

First, when a manufacturer of physical goods adjusts production to meet consumer preferences, the manufacturer does so on an aggregate basis in response to aggregate demand. But there must be individual responses to individual service needs. Second, there is a disparity of power between large service organizations and individuals who need services. As noted in Chapter 2, personnel in service organizations are "gatekeepers of society," with power to exclude individuals who displease them from society as a whole. Third, compulsions like compulsory school attendance suppress the voices of individual needs. Fourth, the market mechanism lacks economic teeth. When an older Indian with swollen feet was asked why he did not visit the clinic, he responded, "I would just have to sit there two days before anyone would see me and then they would say they have to cut my feet off." Later, his prediction came true, because his diabetes had been untreated too long. But as far as the clinic was concerned, from an economic point of view it had simply attracted a surgical customer instead of a medical one.

Productive means fruitful, fertile, creative. Being productive means accomplishing or achieving. Productivity in service organizations involves both the efficiency with which resources are used and the effectiveness of the services rendered. Although manufacturers and merchandisers of physical goods appear to achieve effectiveness without a Target Model, in Chapter 3 we saw that service organizations without a Target Model have low or negative effectiveness. Although profit-making organizations can use profits in a competitive marketplace as their chosen measurement of productivity, multiple measurements should be used, because measurements control objectives and results. If output per working hour is used as the sole or principal measurement of productivity, for example, the consequence will be displacement of people from organizations and organizational effectiveness will be ignored, at least in service organizations.

Both profit and nonprofit organizations can measure productivity in terms of annual rates of change, which is the way cost of living is measured. Using subjective as well as objective measurements, not only overall productivity but changes in the separate elements of efficiency and effectiveness can be measured this way. Measuring change makes improvement the objective, gives support to processes of Developing and Achieving in Complete Organizations, and helps the bosses rationalize their control of the passage between the Established and the Target Models to improve both efficiency and effectiveness concurrently.

DEALING WITH LOW-GRADED PEOPLE

"Service organizations are filled with people who are not capable of personal development," a consultant has said, "and furthermore such people do not want to develop." Any manager or teacher can observe confirming evidence for this statement, and it is surely an exercise in futility to clear the passage to the Target Model for those who will not take a single step toward development on their own volition. The problem is pervasive, and there are answers to it in organizational and motivational theory which this book rejects.

Erich Fromm, I believe, has said, "Man has only one real interest and that is the full development of his potentialities, of himself as a human being." What happened to the people observed by Fromm that turned them into the people encountered by managers and teachers? (See Figure 10-1.)

FIGURE 10-1
Low-Graded People

When organizations move down the Hierarchy
of Methods people go down too.

In the 1800's before the Federal Government took control of
Cherokee affairs, the tribe had "an educational system which
produced a Cherokee population 90 percent literate in its native
language and used bilingual materials to such an extent that
Oklahoma Cherokees had a higher English literacy level than the
white populations of either Texas or Arkansas." Now, "the
median number of school years completed by the adult Cherokee
population is only 5.5; 40 percent of adult Cherokees are func-
tionally illiterate; Cherokee dropout rates in public schools is as
high as 75 percent; and the level of Cherokee education is well
below the average for rural and nonwhites in the State."

Source: Indian Education: A National Tragedy—A National Challenge, 1969
Report of the U.S. Senate Committee on Labor and Public Welfare, p. 19.

Perceptions and Self-Perceptions

In Established Model Organizations managers and teachers see only incomplete people, because their organizations have slots for only parts of people. Members of minority races wear masks through which establishment managers and teachers are allowed to see only the stereotypes the establishment requires them to see. Never volunteer, never question, never admit to knowledge outside one's place are survival rules, especially for low-graded people in Established Model Organizations. Diagnoses follow the system's needs, so those for whom the system has no jobs are diagnosed as unemployable and those for whom there are only low-graded jobs are labeled incapable of development. Because the diagnoses of the system correlate so well with the realities which unfortunate people must endure, the diagnoses tend to be incorporated as self-perceptions.

Development ceases to the degree that individuals have been conditioned to feel that their efforts are futile and that they are helpless to determine their own futures. Rats that have been tied and given repeated electric shocks do not try to escape the shocks when their bonds are removed. Freedom and opportunity do not restart the Development process, but merely make it possible for reverse conditioning to restart the process. The contra to rejection is not indifference or neutrality, but acceptance.

Whatever the degree to which people have been conditioned to being hopeless, helpless, and nondevelopmental, a service organization must not treat them as permanently disabled. There is always a next step for everyone as long as there is life, and dispensing kindness and watered-down tasks is the ultimate contempt. Productivity in a service organization improves only as each person in the organization takes his or her next step. Members of the group must walk together. Toughness in enforcing the responsibilities of associates rather than kindness in tolerating the incapacities of subordinates is the organizational necessity. Neither discrimination nor reverse discrimination is involved when this approach is followed, but sensitive perception of next steps is required.

Stages of Development

Psychologists tell us that stages of development are in fixed sequence like the rungs of a ladder. As mothers know, children play alone before they play in parallel and they play in parallel before they interact. There are analogies for work. Erickson[2] tells us that autonomy precedes initiative and that there is a transitional confusion in passing from individual identity to role, from independence to interdependence and fusion. Generativity appears to be the highest of Erickson's operational stages, but he adds that there must be an integrated system which can be trusted. Trust in the system is a prerequisite for any development at all in new members of an organization.

"Out of sight, out of mind" is a characteristic of one of the early stages of development identified by Piaget.[3] Industrial workers on assembly lines are frozen at this stage, as are office workers when they are restricted to performing only the operations that move papers across their desks from in-boxes to out-boxes. Purposeful action is at a later stage, to be followed by a stage at which explanations are called for. New employees often ask questions prematurely, before they have moved through the stages which must precede useful questions. Poor timing results in apparently stupid questions, followed in sequence by humiliating responses, a tendency to hold back further questions, and a freezing of development at an early stage. In Established Model Organizations this result is welcomed, but in Complete Organizations steps must be taken to avoid it.

If service organizations are in fact filled with people incapable of developing and entering the Target Model, we must recognize organizational processes as the cause and not inherent inadequacies of people. (See Figure 10-1.) By altering processes we can help people take their next steps, however painful they may be, and only then will the productivity of service organizations improve.

CHOOSING A SYMBOLIC MATRIX

Our actions tend to conform to our mental model of what our actions should be. The symbolic representation of an organization, therefore, tends to control the behavior and interactions of those who recognize and understand the symbol. The Established Organization symbol is a pyramid, seen traditionally as a naked hierarchy of authority but with apologists who see it as clothed in kindly motivation. Most people know the pyramid symbol and have been schooled to conform their behavior to its shape.

The hourglass shape, which was illustrated in Chapter 8 (Figure 8-1) and discussed earlier in this chapter, is important because, unless we model our behavior to conform to its shape, we cannot develop and achieve a Complete Organization. Without the hourglass symbol, supervisors say, "What else is there to do except tell people what to do, teach them, and motivate them?" Using the wrong map or symbol keeps us from moving toward our objectives regardless of idealism, necessity, or determination. Using the right map or symbol does not guarantee an easy trip, but it does make progress and achievement possible.

A third symbol is also needed, because as organizations grow they must evolve new structures and patterns of interacting.

Limits to Size

There are limits to the size of Complete Organizations. The limits may be physical, like the decreasing proportion of surface cells to interior cells when size increases, unless an organization becomes convoluted like a human brain. The limits may be functional, like loss of precision when a cutting edge enlarges from scalpel to butcher's knife to axe. The limits may be adaptive, like the decreasing range of suitable environments when animals increase in size from fly to deer to elephant or whale.

How large can an organization be and still function as a team? A basketball team has five players, a surgical team six or eight, and a football team eleven. With alternates, understudies, and specialists, perhaps we can have teams with thirty or forty members or even more. If we assume that team limits apply to the Target Model and Complete Organizations, what kind of an organization is a hospital with over a thousand employees and how can we diagram it?

Conventionally, large organizations have been symbolized by the pyramid of authority, which can be expanded indefinitely as size increases: one guard for five prisoners; one sergeant and two guards for ten prisoners; one lieutenant, two sergeants, and four guards for twenty prisoners, and so on ad infinitum. A large university can be symbolized by twelve such steps from teaching assistants up to chancellor at the apex. Fortunately for humanity and for productivity in service organizations, there is an alternative symbol and alternative reality.

Matrix Organizations

A matrix is that which gives origin or form to a thing, or which serves to enclose it. Universities, hospitals, and other large service organizations are usefully visualized as Matrix Organizations which create, guide, and provide support systems for the organs and organizational units within them. Thus a Matrix Organization determines the interrelated missions and models of its internal units and allocates resources to them. Hierarchical management in a pyramid matrix creates an impossible environment for internal units that are Complete Organizations. A rectangular, circular, or irregular matrix, however, can be a fertile field in which productive internal units can grow.

An army general deploys troops and is concerned with the logistics of supporting them in accordance with their missions. When a famous general became president of a great university in the Far East, he exercised a major influence on the budgetary process of allocating resources, but he did not set up a conventional chain of command and take on a command function for himself. His concern was to form Complete Organization units within the matrix of the university.

How does management develop and maintain a Matrix Organization for productivity in providing services to people? It uses all methods in the Hierarchy of Organization Methods, not just authority. It provides supply and communication systems and allocates resources. It releases its internal units to take on hourglass configurations instead of confining them to pyramids. It obligates all members of the organization to take their next steps so all can walk together.

CONCLUSION

The greater the circle of the known, the greater the circle of the unknown. Thus each new answer or idea is the basis for a new question. In turn, each new answer-question couplet can be the basis for a working hypothesis to test in life. With the basic structure or theme of the book completed at this point, the next chapter describes three tests of working hypotheses derived from the material presented.

NOTES

[1] Laurence Peter and Raymond Hall, *The Peter Principle*, Bantam Books, Inc., New York, 1970.

[2] Erik Erickson, quoted in Helen G. Westlake, *Relationship: A Study in Human Behavior*, Ginn & Company, Boston, 1969, Chapter 34.

[3] Jean Piaget, quoted in John L. Phillips, Jr., *The Origins of Intellect—Piaget's Theory*, W. H. Freeman and Company, San Francisco, 1969, Chapter 2.

ELEVEN

Three Extended Examples

We are ineffective if we perceive and react only to structures, people, actions, or events. Unless we also perceive and react to processes, we may sell ourselves for kind words from a hierarchical superior who is rejecting us. We will be unable to move ourselves and the institutions of which we are a part up the Hierarchy of Organization Methods. Processes in the real world are invisible, however, unless we see them first as perception models in the mind. Three extended examples are given in this chapter to add dimensions to our models.

CHANGES IN THE COMPTROLLER'S OFFICE
OF THE FOUNDATION

In 1957, at the end of my first term as treasurer of the New Jersey Society of CPA's, its trustees revised the budgets to conform to the penny with actual expenditures. Similarly, in 1965 when I became comptroller of The Rockefeller Foundation, budgets were revised at year-end to cover overexpenditures, and the bank accounts of overseas field directors were reimbursed only when banks gave notice the accounts were overdrawn. Accounting in nonprofit organizations, including governments, was more concerned with appropriations and commitments than with responsibility and performance. The by-laws of the Foundation charged the comptroller's office with no more than bookkeeping for grants and expenditures, and in 1965 the staff did a minimum of analysis, interpreting, and reporting, no systems work, no tax work, no cost accounting, no auditing, and, of course, no budgetary control.

To get the payroll paid and the voucher checks written and recorded, there were thirty-odd people in thirteen separate sections. Although some had college degrees, only one had taken a semester of college accounting. Specifications for hiring were a high school diploma and ability to type, but several months were usually required to find anyone to fill a vacancy. Someone who took a mathematics course at night was told that that showed lack of interest and attention to his job.

There were over sixteen hundred general ledger accounts and occasionally a trial balance was attempted on a long adding machine tape. Commitment records were not self-correcting and could not be proved routinely. Delays in paying invoices from suppliers and shippers resulted in a steady stream of second and third requests, giving rise to much special handling and twenty or more duplicate payments a month. There were three kinds of backlogs in the department's day-to-day work: (1) external—for example, the field office reports of local expenditures and foreign bank balances averaged six months' delay and some were over a year in arrears; (2) procedural—for example, to issue a foreign draft involved more than twenty steps requiring one to two weeks' time; and (3) clerical—for example, expense reports piled up for weeks or even months before being processed.

The comptroller of another major foundation explained nonprofit accounting to me: "Constantly raise questions about little items, but never about anything big. Be sticky about approvals, but never about concept or purpose." Only yesterday he must have talked to the comptrollers of your hometown, the CIA, and many major universities. All this is clear enough in retrospect, but my expectations had been naïve. Reality showed up one piece at a time, obliterating any dream of a neatly ordered professional existence.

Getting Started

As a first step in bringing the full range of comptrollership functions into the department, I pushed to have bank reconciliations transferred from the treasurer's office. It was a fortunate mistake because it taught me early not to ask for work until we had the time and skills to do it. After a few months the reconciliations were back in the treasurer's office and reality was being confronted: "Today, none of us has the skills which will be needed for employment here five years from now." New measurements were being defined: "There are no deadlines as long as the rate of progress is satisfactory." The Target Model was being forced into existence: "Those of us who do not continually grow into new responsibilities will go." Four strenuous years later, we started to install a computer, using our own personnel all the way.

Trying to find names for the processes that were going on helped in mastering them and applying them consistently. For example, system and control improvements may bring to light errors and problems that had formerly been buried. Within and without the department there were those who said that each change was for the worse because of the errors and problems it gave rise to. Especially at the interface of the department with program officers and other administrative officers, I felt a tension in this regard. Good personal relations with peers and superiors in a hierarchy are easy if the game is played of ascribing errors to the lowest clerks. But exercising authority by assigning blame downward and setting limits of tolerance improves nothing unless we assume Theory X subordinates Organizational productivity as distinct from individual performance can be improved only by dealing with errors at the highest level of procedure, policy, or system within or without a department. "Converting people problems to work problems" became the guide to responsible behavior as well as a comfortable rationalization for any personal ineptness.

Standard approaches for improving office efficiency include (1) improvement in management by use of work schedules and flexible work assignments, (2) improvement in work patterns by skill development and use of work-simplification techniques, (3) revisions of systems and procedures, and (4) introduction of machine accounting. These methods could not be applied from the top down unless it was possible to obtain a quick return, because their use added work before reducing it. They could be applied from the bottom up, however, by anyone who chose to use them. To encourage their use, questions were asked and new patterns of perception were promoted.

A routine office problem is selection of the best method of communication: face-to-face, interoffice phone, or interoffice mail. If the wrong patterns are established, it can be costly. For example, it was observed that one employee started spending several hours each day at other desks waiting for information and approvals in order to expedite special work. It was a normal, unskilled reaction to pressure, so general discussion was promoted rather than dealing with the one visible instance. Nonetheless, I was irritated enough to express some personal reactions and give the employee an Avis button saying, "We try harder." The next day the employee reported a nightmare and I had to fall back on our guideline that in the office we were concerned only with work problems, not personal ones.

To improve productivity, it is sometimes helpful to estimate potential gains. So how about looking at things this way? We work 75 percent of office time. Only 75 percent of our work is worth doing and our procedures are only 75 percent efficient. Our output is thus 37½ percent and our first goal is 50 percent. This was too much for most to accept, but it did help to refocus attention to payoff areas.

A nonstandard method of achieving immediate gains in output, without investment of preliminary time or effort, was fortuitously discovered and was applied with Authority. The method which is still nameless was nothing more than the converse application of an unpublished law of productivity, to wit, inefficiency begets inefficiency. As a simple example, when clerks were observed searching for something in a pile of unfiled material, they were reassigned to filing. On a more sophisticated level, when it was determined that handling second and third requests for payment consumed most of the time of a clerk, the clerk was reassigned to processing original invoices. Unfortunately, the method could be applied only when complete elimination of a backlog could be quickly achieved.

Installing a Computer

By 1969, we were ready to shoot for bringing in a computer late in 1970. Doing it ourselves would carry a heavy price tag—more than a 50 percent increase in workload for at least two years without additional personnel. Even after computer applications appeared to be running well, we would expect to play safe by keeping up the old manual records in parallel for six months or a year. Despite the costs and risks we foresaw, a consensus grew that bringing in a computer was a natural step in our organizational and individual processes of developing. Placing the order was not a decision, but merely a formal ratification that a consensus had emerged.

On July 1, 1969, a contract was signed and four people were transferred from processing daily work to developing program specifications and learning how to program. The internal auditor started a major concentration on controls needed for computer operations, and the tax accountant started to detail his requirement for each projected application. Section supervisors and assistant supervisors began courses so they could be active participants and responsible for their records after computerization. Above all, their need was to control output. In manual and mechanical record-keeping systems, human intelligence can be applied to the data item by item as calculations are made. In computerized systems, the supervisor is presented with a pile of completed checks, registers, and records to be challenged for reasonableness, tested for completeness, and proved by totals and by process reviews.

Step by step we were vulnerable to criticism. We missed target dates for new applications. The proficiencies of our programmers were obviously limited, and programs that ran could be seen to be cumbersome and inefficient. Keypunch operators promoted to computer operators had to learn as they produced. There was only one defense, but it was intriguing. Two years after the computer was delivered, there had been sufficient reduction in staff (by attrition) to cover the cost of computer rental. Today the operation is still vulnerable to criticism and still improving, handling more volume, absorbing new work, and carrying out special assignments without a whimper.

Another place had consultants do feasibility studies and, on the basis of their information and recommendations, top management made the decision to bring in a computer. A new department was set up and skilled personnel were hired to staff it, but most programming was contracted out on the theory that once programs are written, the need for programmers is gone. The original staff in the comptroller's office continued unreduced in numbers and nonparticipants in the computer operations, although the computer department was soon given to the comptroller to supervise. It was a beautiful installation, efficient in every way and approved by every expert who reviewed it. When top management decreed a general budget cutback, the staff of the comptroller's office, which had doubled, was ordered cut in half, and customers were sought for the excess capacity of the computer. Unfortunately there were too few trained programmers on the staff to make all the necessary system modifications.

"The conclusion to be drawn from your computer installation story," some managers in the Established Model have told me, "is that your office was incredibly inefficient to begin with and some of its operations still are. For example, you still type checks manually and then keypunch the data to get it on the computer. Eliminate that duplication and overall your department will gain 3 percent in efficiency." Among those who have not understood the process is my friend who was ordered to cut his staff in half. His computer prints his checks.

Problems with Roles

In a Complete Organization the supervisor must function in both models, Target and Established, like the mediator-arbitrator of the National Center for Dispute Settlement. What is the role of a supervisor in the Target Model? As the comptroller's office moved up the Hierarchy of Organization Methods, the role of a supervisor in the Target Model grew faster than our understanding of it. "Think of yourself as coordinator instead of boss," was one attempt to guide. The word *coordinator*, however, refers to only one of the six processes in the Target Model, and a supervisor must use all six when in that model. Without doubt, the greatest brake on progress was lack of a comprehensive description for supervisors of the kind of organization we should be and how they should function in it.

Using responsibility instead of authority as our guide, we made the tax accountant, internal auditor, and systems manager direct-line participants instead of staff advisors. For all nonroutine work, a special form was devised to elicit input. The chief accountant stated the level of reporting, like rounding to the nearest thousand dollars. The internal auditor defined controls. The systems manager stated how to do it, and the senior supervisor stated when and by whom it should be done. Then the designated section supervisor accepted or refused responsibility for the work as specified. Finally the comptroller or assistant comptroller gave approval or refusal for the expenditure of time involved. Beautiful in theory, but in practice many expressed any bright idea that entered their heads regardless of whether or not it was within role. It is not easy to learn to mind one's own role. In the Established Model, we must remember, the rewards go to the person who does the most upstaging, most subordinating of others, and most directing of them in their business.

Years ago when I was in public accounting and writing a book on auditing, I asked an assistant what a supervisor should do. "Be used" was his answer, which meant, in the parlance of this book, get with the Target Model. Years later he reminisced over lunch, "For Supervisor A I worked hard because he scared me, for B I worked hard because he was such a nice guy, and for C because I knew it was for my own good." The real problem, however, was not to get him to work hard, but to get him and us to work more effectively, to develop and achieve. For the latter purpose, neither the authority of A nor the personality of B would suffice. Improved productivity in organizations and improved effectiveness of individuals in their roles are derived from mastering of methods and processes, not from fear or praise, the stick or the carrot.

Unconclusion

After ten years (see Figure 11-1), the comptroller's office is back to doing bank reconciliations, is responsible for financial reporting, and is starting to make scheduled visits to grantees. One-third of the staff is now doing the clerical work that, in the past, took two-thirds of the staff. Another third of the staff is doing analytical, technical, and professional work that, in the past, had not been done at all. Minorities are now the majority in the department. There are no dead-end jobs, but neither are there formal career ladders. Maintaining consensus and momentum on indi-

FIGURE 11-1

Office History

Highlights and trends in the comptroller's office.

	Training	*Reports and analyses*
1965	Sept.—10 staff started at night college.	
1966	Jan.—6 staff to data processing school at night for semester. June—2 staff to IBM training center for five weeks.	9/1—Started monthly statements.
1967	In-house courses in controls for most of staff. In-house typing class. 27 staff members in night college courses.	1/1—Started monthly reports to directors. 9/1—New coding manual six pages in length. PATMAN REPORT
1968	10 staff members in data processing courses at night colleges. 10 staff members in other night college courses.	PATMAN REPORT Revised coding manual eight pages in length.
1969	10 staff members in night college courses. 33 staff members for aggregate of 73 weeks at UNIVAC.	1/1—Revised coding manual 20 pages 2/17—Apptd. Chief Acct. 9/1—New shipping report. 10/1—PETERSON COMMISSION REPORT
1970	19 staff members for aggregate of 23 weeks at UNIVAC.	1/1—Revised coding manual 26 pages. 1/1—Tax Reform Act. Integrated tax requirements into record keeping and control activities.

Controls	Systems and equipment
1/1—Established control accounts and formal *subsidiary ledgers.* 7/1—Started monthly trial balances.	4/1—New check voucher. 7/1—Comptroller's Office responsible for data processing equipment.
Sept.—Elimination of most clerical backlogs. 11/8—New position—Tax Accountant. Dec.—Internal audit of centers in Colombia.	1/1—New Ass't. Comptroller with competence in teaching and systems. Started general ledger on tab equipment, other procedures revised.
1/1—New budgetary controls. 1/1—Direct controls over program center cash. 1/1—New position—Internal Auditor. 1/1—Match invoices and PO's.	1/1—New budget revision procedures. New forms, checklists, work schedules, etc. 10/15—Appointment of Computer Consultant.
Continuing extension of budgetary controls. Requested continuing suggestions from CPAs on computer. 11/1—Set up control unit for input, processing, and output controls for documentation and operating control maintenance.	3/22—Specification to computer manufacturer. 7/1 —Selection of UNIVAC. Phase One Applications 11/3—Computer delivery.

FIGURE 11-1 (*continued*)

Office History

Highlights and trends in the comptroller's office.

	Training	*Reports and analyses*
1971	12 staff members for aggregate of 19 weeks at UNIVAC. Increased participation of staff in professional and technical societies.	Improved analysis of grantees' financial reports.
1972	15 staff members in night courses.	Wage stabilization analyses. New 990 and pension reports. Historical summaries by area of interest.
1973	14 staff members in night college courses. Improved procedural writeups and job descriptions.	Cost benefit analysis of RF Illustrated. First steps toward program budgets. Change to accrual basis.
1974	17 staff members in night college courses. Attendance at professional meetings and conferences.	New records and reports required for employee benefits.
1975	14 staff members in night college courses. Special in-house training on new pension law.	New responsibility for general financial reporting. Expanded budget system and program budgeting.

peredThree Extended Examples 193

Controls		Systems and equipment
Incorporated tax reviews in control schedules.		General ledger, etc. on computer, start of expenditure history file. Parallel running of payroll.
Visits to financial offices of five grantees.		N.Y. payroll on computer. General retrieval system. Declinations, etc. on computer.
Computer tape library fully functioning. Formalized programs for internal auditing.		Field staff payroll, appropriations, and reports on computer. American Music history project on computer.
Visits to overseas programs and grantees in Africa and Asia. Control of general files and start of report library. Increased attention to administrative needs of grantees. Bank reconciliations.		Variety of special projects on computer.
		Faster printer, three-year contract renewal. Planning re needs for three years hence.

FIVE-YEAR COMPUTER CONTRACT UNIVAC 9200-II

vidual and organizational developing and achieving seems to require continuous awareness and responsiveness instead of set patterns.

Ten years from now the status indicated in the preceding paragraph should be the before part in another before-and-after story.

ROLES AND JOBS IN
PENSION ADMINISTRATION

With inflation at 7 percent, prices double in ten years and quadruple in twenty. So a pension with a cost-of-living escalator must be fantastically expensive. Wrong. One year after I realized that inflation is not a cost but a means of transferring wealth, The Rockefeller Foundation made an almost no-cost amendment to its pension plan, providing an automatic, open-ended cost-of-living escalator. While the amendment was being developed, I learned a lot about the roles of insurance companies and trust departments and the jobs of people in them. For example, insurance companies have moved away from insurable risks, as far as pensions are concerned, avoiding responsibility for effective service by passing on some of the biggest risks to their annuitants.

> Rockefeller Foundation can afford to meet the unknown financial obligations of a formula benefit plan related to final average salary, and even the costs of being committed in perpetuity to cost-of-living increases. Most colleges, universities and schools cannot and should not. Nor have many private pension plans in business and industry, except for a few union-negotiated plans, taken on the cost-of-living commitment. [1]

Obviously, if organizations should not take on the risk of inflation in pensions, the risk must be dumped on retired individuals. It is not to the Established Model that one can look for help in instituting responsible improvements.

> *An Indexed Pension Plan at Low Cost.* It sounds like an impossible dream—a pension that is designed to go up with the consumer price index but has a fixed predetermined cost. Consider, however, this paragraph which appeared in a

speech by Paul H. Jackson of the Wyatt Company before the American Pension Conference on March 12, 1974: "As to the mathematics of funding, I think any good actuary can esti- mate what the cost would be for a consumer price indexed benefit. Actually, here you are estimating the net result of both interest and the CPI [consumer price index] and since we can't estimate closely what the interest rate is going to be alone, there is good reason why we should try to estimate the net total of the two."

Restated, this is a concept that true interest in the absence of inflation is about 3 percent. When inflation is 4 percent, interest should then be 7 percent. When inflation is 15 percent to 18 percent, as it was in Colombia, South America, a few years ago, then interest rates are correspondingly higher.

Applying the Idea. Assume it takes $100,000 to buy one of our retired employees an annuity of $8500. Another way of saying this is that the present value of an annuity of $8500 is $100,000. If we want to increase the annuity 1 percent, we have to increase the cost or present value 1 percent. If we want to increase the annuity 5 percent, we have to increase the cost or present value 5 percent. Where does the extra money come from to cover the increased cost and provide the increased annuity? One source of extra money is investment earnings in excess of the rate used as an actuarial assumption.

Now assume that we fund our annuity on a 3 percent reserve basis. If there is no inflation, our fund should earn "true interest" of 3 percent. If there is 1 percent inflation, we should expect to earn interest of 4 percent and thus have 1 percent extra money to increase the annuity 1 percent. If inflation is 5 percent, we should expect to earn interest of 8 percent and thus have enough extra money to increase the annuity 5 percent. If an organization keeps the extra earnings for itself and pays only a fixed pension to its retired people, it gains for itself dollar for dollar what its pensioners lose.

Problems. What are the arguments against constructing a pen- sion plan on this theory? First is the argument that there is no such thing as "true interest." This argument asserts Paul Jackson was wrong in saying that actuaries can estimate the net difference between interest and inflation. A variant of the argument is that there is not a very good correlation between interest rates and inflation. The organization that uses this argument is probably trying to justify its right to keep for itself its investment earnings over 3 percent—its right to gain as its pensioners lose the purchasing power of their pensions. An efficient manager holds costs down.

A second argument is that funding on a 3 percent reserve basis is too costly. Thus, if you presently assume 5 percent investment earnings, the additional cost of switching to a 3 percent assumption is 14 percent. But it is not a 14 percent increase in plan costs. It is only an increase in cost for employees already retired. The pension fund and pension costs can be visualized to have two parts—accruals for active employees and a separate fund for employees already retired. Furthermore, we found the cost of an annuity on a 3 percent basis is almost identical with the cost of an equity annuity. If an organization stays with the 5 percent assumption, however, it should also state that its 2 percent inflation assumption also applies to the purchasing power of the pension being offered. There must be consistency in the economic data used in actuarial assumptions.

A third argument deals with mortality risk. Since no insurance company presently offers a contract in this form, the employer must take on mortality risk. We were told that many employers cannot and should not take on the financial risk of having their annuitants live too long. And it gave us pause until we realized that the risk could be measured fairly easily.

The following calculations show the difference between annuities and straight interest as to annual yield from $10,000. They also indicate the relative risk from self-insurance of an annuitant "living too long."

Ten-Year Life Expectancy, 3% Interest

Annuity	$1,172	391%
Interest	300	100
Self-Insurance Risk		291%

Twenty-five–Year Life Expectancy, 8% Interest

Annuity	$ 937	117%
Interest	800	100
Self-Insurance Risk		17%

Thirty-Year Life Expectancy, 10% Interest

Annuity	$1,061	106%
Interest	1,000	100
Self-Insurance Risk		6%

The ten-year life expectancy, 3 percent interest assumption was appropriate several decades ago, but not today. With joint and survivor annuities and earlier retirement, the middle assumption is more reasonable. Mortality risk is peanuts compared to inflation risk!

A fourth argument is that the theory is hard to explain and leaves the employee with increases dependent on investment performance. So we pegged the benefit formula in our plan to the prime rate instead of to actual investment earnings. An analysis showed, to our satisfaction, that automatic turning over of high-grade commercial paper would result in earning the prime rate less a percent or half a percent. In other words, we could cope with the investment risk and give the retired employee an independent measure of pension increases. (Our old annuity contracts with the insurance company, however, guaranteed only 2½ percent interest with dividends, if any, depending on policies and votes of a board of directors as well as investment performance.) Yes, pensions involve complex considerations, but we found our staff was ready to study and consider and was quick to understand.

The formula we finally adopted was an annual increase in the pension after retirement calculated in two steps. Step one is a guaranteed annual increase up to the first 4 percent increase in the consumer price index. Step two is to match increases in the index above 4 percent, but only if the total increase in the annuity does not exceed the average prime rate for the year less 3 percent. Since 1955 our formula would have covered about 90 percent of the increase in the consumer price index. The trustees of the Foundation approved the indexed pension in connection with other changes that added up to a no-cost package.

Conclusion. Unlike other improvements in a pension plan, to index benefits does not change anything except the measuring stick we use. Added benefits result in added costs, but in a real sense indexing a plan is not adding a benefit. Rather it is a commitment not to take away in the event of inflation a benefit already provided by changing the measuring stick. Our approach was not to shift risks and avoid responsibilities. Instead, we sought to analyze and control the risks and to define and assign the responsibilities.

Who Is Minding the Store?

Investment managers are rated by comparing the earnings of their funds with the earnings of other funds. Their goal is to beat the averages, not to achieve the best correlation of yield with inflation. They make no guarantees, and from the consumer's viewpoint, as many of them will earn below the averages as will earn above. In the Established Model successful fund managers are highly compensated under the star system and have no incentive for steady, unspectacular responsible performance which delivers inflation protection to pensioners by earning the prime rate year after year. Fund managers can be given the incentive and assigned the responsibility to implement a pension plan keyed to the cost-of-living index, but it is naïve to think they would take the initiative to change the game in which their personal stakes are highest.

Actuaries are experts in mathematics, but as to pensions, the essence of their roles is to manipulate and integrate assumptions—assumptions as to mortality, investment earnings, future salary levels, how many will retire early, how many will leave before pension rights are vested, and so on. Since assumptions about the future control our behavior more than knowledge about the past, actuaries are very powerful indeed. In insurance companies they commonly hold high executive positions. In TIAA/ CREF, as the earlier quotation shows, they are openly paternalistic, saying what the colleges and universities they serve can and should do. Like parents resisting the new worlds and values of their children, actuaries, or some of them, can be expected to resist the new needs of those they are supposed to serve.

Administrators of pensions are required by law to be "corrupt" and to resist all change. The legal mechanism by which pension administrators are locked into the established order is the statutory imposition of the "prudent man" standard. This standard holds administrators responsible in piecemeal fashion, decision by decision and action by action, for doing what other established administrators would have done under the same circumstances. To have the courage of one's convictions and to act according to one's belief is to ignore the standard at one's peril. To innovate and do something different is to fail the standard. It is not to administrators that one can look for either initiation or support of constructive change.

How the Foundation Plan Got Through

The Rockefeller Foundation adopted its indexed pension plan not as a big decision but as an unconclusion, as part of a process of developing, adapting, and achieving. Five times since 1946, when a long-service secretary retired on a monthly pension of $80, the Foundation increased the pensions of its retired personnel to offset inflation. Among the trustees who voted the increases were industrialists who had done the same in corporations that they headed.

At first, the Foundation had a defined contribution pension plan of the type still prevalent in colleges, paying each month a percentage of each employee's salary into an individual annuity contract. This accumulated for the employee a retirement fund related to the price and salary levels of his or her working years. To protect pension expectations from erosion by inflation before retirement, the Foundation added a guarantee that someone with thirty years of service would retire on a pension of no less than half his or her final average salary. Refinements to the guarantee evolved into a complete shift to a defined benefit or formula benefit plan. Then the plan was revised to fund part of each new pension in an equity annuity which would fluctuate with the stock market and, despite the risks involved, would provide the best available protection against inflation after retirement. As inflation increased, interest earned on fixed annuity funds also increased, so it was possible to offer retiring employees a new option without additional cost to the Foundation—a fixed annuity that automatically increased 3 percent a year, compounded. About two years later the plan was revised again to provide the new automatic, open-ended cost-of-living escalator.

As a result of this continuing process of improvement, and there were many other pension elements in the process, costs today are less than if the plan of fifteen years ago were still in effect unchanged. The most expensive pension plan is the one that does not do its job, just as the most expensive medical plan is the one that pays for unnecessary surgery or other unproductive health care.

The indexed plan got through not only because of the process, but also because the Foundation is a *Complete Organization,* structured on responsibilities as well as on orders and decisions, with Target Model areas as well as areas of the Established Model. In the Target Model was a role with responsibility for employee benefits. Within the role there was a team, myself and others in the comptroller's office, our counsel and our actuary. Protected by the role, which we had created for ourselves, any criticism or hostility of others served only to test and refine our work instead of to threaten our jobs. So we sought out other views and benefited from them. In the end, this more than anything helped us keep the process going. The process in the people, in the team, in the role, and in the Target Model structure of the Complete Organization was how the plan got through.

MODELS AND PROCESSES
IN AN URBAN COMMUNITY COLLEGE[2]

Give a Target Model mission to an Established Model Organization and either the mission or the organization must change. When open admissions was stated by the Board of Higher Education to be the policy of the City University of New York, events followed a predictable sequence. The senior colleges agreed that every high school graduate deserved a chance to go to college, but not at the cost of lowering institutional standards. So the admissions plan stipulated that students graduating with averages 80 or above could enter the senior colleges and all others would be allocated to the community colleges.

Roughly ten years after its birth, Manhattan Community College had 10,000 full-time students. At the midpoint of this life span, the open-admissions policy had been adopted and incoming students became mostly lower-ranking and mostly ethnic minorities. Faculty members were engulfed by drastic changes in their work environment, both cultural and academic. Student disturbances, including occupation of the president's office, led to closing of the school. The president resigned. The successor pres-

FIGURE 11-2

A Rehabilitation Team

The makeup of the team varies with the patient's needs. The nurse, the patient, and the doctor are always members.

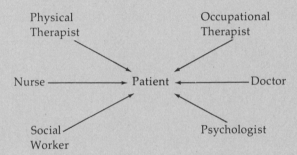

The nurse has a special responsibility for making the patient part of the team. "The practice of nursing as a registered nurse is defined as diagnosing and treating human responses to actual and potential health problems." (New York State, Nurse Practice Act, 1972.)

"Because of her intimate knowledge of the patient, she plays a vital part in helping to coordinate and plan the care given to him by members of the rehabilitation team." (*IRM*, 1974, a publication of the Institute of Rehabilitation Medicine, New York University Medical Center.)

The registered nurse has to work in the Target Model—seeking consensus, accepting, coordinating, testing, interpreting, giving of understanding, and feeding back. Not that the nurse is supposed to abstain from Force and Authority. The role is a full one.

ident, the college's third in less than five years, was black, guile-less, and committed. Ordered to reopen the school, he acted decisively and forcefully.

With the school reopened, he moved to organize the resources of the school around its students in the same way that a rehabilita-tion team is organized around its patients (see, for example, Fig-ure 11-2). As a starter, he charged the faculty with sensitivity and responsiveness to the varying needs of the students. It was a bold essential step. Either the school would change to Target Model processes in support of open admissions or the school would stay in the Established Model and the open-admissions policy would be twisted or aborted. As one could predict, the central office establishment imposed a policy of testing all incoming students and assigning them to remediation classes until they met conven-tional admission standards. The result was to segregate open-admission students, mainly black and Puerto Rican, from the rest of the student body. The president vainly urged consideration of the adverse educational impacts of this policy. An attempt by him to give some measure of responsibility to the students by means of group counseling was crushed by an order from headquarters to give each student individual direction. When it reached the point that 90 percent of the incoming students at Manhattan Commu-nity College were required to take remediation courses, it could be said with some truth that open admissions had been twisted to mean freedom to repeat the last year of high school.

Scapegoating

"It strikes us that the conventional approach for helping higher education has focused largely on structure. In most of the case studies we have seen, however, it has been strong leaders who have most determined the success or failure of the projects."[3] Either structure or people must always seem the issue to those who have no perceptiveness for processes. At Manhattan Com-munity College when higher authority acted to keep the school in the Established Model with boundaries and structure unchanged, all the problems of urban education that were funneled to the school had to be seen by those who do not see processes as matters of the personality and competence of the new president. Saul

Alinsky understood how the establishment acts: personalize the issues, he advised, instead of attacking policies or institutions.[4] As an agent of change, the new president was attacked from above and below. The real accomplishments of the school and his administration remained invisible.

It is easy to see what any good establishment-type top executive must do in such circumstances: document the case. A team from the chancellor's office reviewed the Borough of Manhattan Community College and prepared a report which was overwhelmingly negative. Instead of wilting under fire, however, the president responded with a spirited defense, challenging both the facts and conclusions in the report prepared by the chancellor's team. Seven months after the review someone leaked the report to *The New York Times,* which published a front-page story under the headline, "Wide Deficiencies Seen at Manhattan Community." Almost simultaneously a new review team moved in. The first draft of its report was not only overwhelmingly negative, but incredibly so.

This time the deans of the college prepared a lengthy and detailed response entitled "Correction of Errors." A group of community representatives who serve as an advisory council to the president studied both the chancellor's report and deans' response. The advisory council, of which I am cochairman, met with the chancellor, requesting an impartial, independent review of the college and pledging support for actions based on such review. For several months thereafter, the council heard nothing, and then someone told a member that the influence of the president had been checked out and he did not have the support of the black community.

Scapegoating or Processes of Improving?

At this point, the advisory council appealed directly to the Board of Higher Education for independent impartial reviews of both the college and the chancellor's office. One board member observed that in a long-standing controversy there is a temptation to ignore the merits and seek a fresh start by getting rid of some central figure. Another reportedly felt that the board had to choose between firing the president and firing the chancellor. Such are the ways of authority in the Established Model. In any event, the board asked the chancellor to submit a formal report on the matter.

The chancellor's report was twenty-two typewritten pages and it was reasonable in terms of the Established Model. It dealt mostly with structural and people problems, acknowledged improvements in many areas, but concluded the president should not have credit for the progress that had been achieved. The basic question was defined not as the current state of the educational program at the college, but whether the chancellor and the board believed the leadership at the college to be adequate to meet the educational and administrative challenges of the future. According to *The New York Times*, the chancellor asserted that an impartial review would be destructive and he recommended that the president be asked to resign.

> "There seems to be a general agreement among educators that there are certain actions and patterns of actions that prevent progress and learning and education. Specifically, people who are made to feel defensive, fearful, attacked, or threatened are effectively blocked from learning and changing and developing. From my contacts with administrators, deans, and some students at the school, there is no doubt in my mind that they feel threatened and defensive and, it seems to me, that their reactions are not unreasonable. Do you agree that certain actions can have the effects that I have stated and that it is reasonable that people at the school would react as they have?" He answered that the principle was valid.

The board did not act on his recommendation but a month or so later announced it would develop criteria or standards for the evaluation of presidents of all community and senior colleges in the City University. Furthermore, it was announced that the President of Manhattan Community College would be the first to be judged when the criteria and review mechanism were established. Meantime, the president was requested to address himself to areas of weakness and deficiency at the college, a list of which would be developed by the chancellor.

What's the Answer?

The advisory council expressed to the board its regret that the president was again placed on the defensive by being given a list of so-called "areas of weakness or deficiency at the college." We had thought that the first purpose of impartial review was to determine if these were, in fact, areas of weakness or deficiency. We also saw grim irony in the fact that the Board of Higher Education was developing standards to be applied retroactively to judge a college president. To manipulate guilt or innocence, passing or failing, is to show concern for the processes of authority rather than processes of education and improvement.

A conceptual framework exists for performance reviews, as the City University should know. One fundamental concept is that the findings be replicable, and from personal experience, we know that valid findings are almost always concurred in by the person or organization being reviewed. Questions of fact should be agreed on during a review. Performance reviews which do not include discussions with those responsible for the work and which leave facts in dispute for months and years afterwards without attempting to reconcile and resolve differences cannot be expected to result in improved performance. Such reviews must be perceived as merely punitive, in effect if not in intent.

There are no answers. But if our goal is improving the productivity of an organization, there are processes to be used. If our goal is to react effectively in a system which judges and tries to reject us, there are processes to be used. To achieve either goal it is futile to personalize the weaknesses of the Established Model by complaining that superiors are unfair or subordinates incompetent. Conversely, to achieve either goal, it is productive to define one's role and to focus on responsibility and performance within that role. Accordingly, the president's advisory council moved to set up distinguished ad hoc committees to define constructive methods of review for each area of so-called weakness in the college. The way to deal with City Hall is not to fight it, but to push it to join us in the Target Model.

SYMBIOSIS

Scientists have identified a variety of arrangements under which different organisms live together, like bacteria in the digestive tracts of deer. Synergistic arrangements enable the different organisms to develop and function better together than apart. Other organizations include those where one kind of organism is inhibited or parasitically drained. A basic book on plant pathology required eight pages to indicate the range of symbiotic relationships,[5] and considerable scientific research is devoted to symbiotic processes. In this book, we have focused on the clusters of processes which make up two basic organizational models. In this chapter, we have presented examples of the intricate interplay of processes in dissimilar situations. Through these examples, we have shown the commonality of patterns which lead to improving organizational productivity and individual effectiveness.

NOTES

[1] Letter of April 16, 1975, from a top executive and actuary of TIAA/CREF (Teachers Insurance and Annuity Association of America and College Retirement Equity Fund), which was sent to me. The description of the indexed pension plan, its concepts, and problems in development, was adapted from articles written for *Pension World* in 1975 and talks given at Employee Benefits Conferences in 1975 in New York, Chicago, Atlanta, Dallas, and San Francisco.

[2] The story about Manhattan Community College, like the story about the comptroller's office, was as seen through my eyes and supported by memory and miscellaneous files. The comptroller's office employed twenty-six student interns from Manhattan Community College over an eight-year span, and I worked closely through these years with Dr. Edward Lewis, Dean of Cooperative Education, and his associates.

[3] An unpublished preliminary report of the International Council for Educational Development to its sponsoring agencies.

[4] Alinsky's advice was given by David Finks, who worked with Alinsky and is writing about his campaigns.

[5] E. C. Stakman and J. George Harrar, *Principles of Plant Pathology*, The Ronald Press Company, New York, 1957.

TWELVE

Recentering and Projection

Individuals are themselves complex organizations with three organizational models—Established, Target, and Complete. As individuals and other complex organizations move up the Hierarchy of Methods, they achieve greater individuality. Their development takes place along a continuum of increasing complexification and interdependence. Regressing down the continuum toward simplification and separation dissipates synergism and severs individuals into hands in a factory and other parts which are as alienated as kidneys in an organ bank.

Parts of individuals fill jobs; complete individuals fill roles. Incomplete organizations have jobs; complete organizations have roles. Individuals are controlled and manipulated by measurements; organizations are controlled and manipulated by measurements. Individuals and the organizations of which they are a part tend to function at the same level. Thus Theory X organizations perceive Theory X employees, students, or citizens, and vice versa. But when individuals assert or organizations demand of them responsible roles, they tend to move together up the Hierarchy of Methods. Conversely, when individuals avoid or organizations deny them responsible roles, they tend to move together downward.

Developing is like virtue, its own reward. Compensation and external rewards tend to hold us where we are. This is not to say that achievement should not be compensated. Developing, however, must be internal and personal and must be achieved at least in part against resistance and despite penalties.

WHAT'S IMPORTANT

With new perception models we have a new world to discover and live in. In the new world are opportunities or demands to work on new important problems. There are new roles for us to create and fill, new skills for us to develop, new priorities for us to establish. Four things that are more important in the new world than in the old are service organizations, productivity, people, and processes.

Service Organizations

Service organizations are important. Armies and navies, symphony orchestras and dance companies, museums and schools. The legislative, judicial, and executive branches of federal, state, and county governments. Municipal water, sanitation, police, fire, and other departments. Unions, professional societies, granges and trade associations, hospitals, nursing homes and public health agencies, prisons, asylums, and other custodial institutions, halfway houses, fraternal, ethnic, youth, and community action groups, architectural, actuarial, and accounting firms, law firms, research institutes, cooperatives, pension trusts, brokerage firms, banks and insurance companies, charities, foundations, and churches.

In the year 1900, total governmental expenditures at all levels in the United States were only 8 percent of the gross national product; in the 1970s, they are more than 33 percent. In the year 1900, the percentage of employment in nonprofit service organizations was negligible; in the 1970s, it is about 30 percent and growing. In the year 1900, the number of college students was less than 100,000; in the 1970s, it is over 8 million. Also in the 1970s, another 40 million students were enrolled in elementary and secondary schools. In the year 1900, most babies were born at home and people avoided hospitals except in extremes; in the 1970s, 15 percent of us enter hospitals each year and hospital clinics have replaced the family doctor.[1]

Service organizations are no longer appendages but the heart and body of the system. They exert control over who lives and the quality of life. They have and use powers which can destroy us, the world in which we live, and the world we leave to those who are yet unborn.

Productivity

Improving the productivity of organizations is important. In the Established Model, medical institutions deliver health injury as well as health care, educational institutions produce more dropouts than graduates, military establishments provide enemies and dangers as well as protection. Penal systems turn out recidivists more efficiently than they lock up criminals, farm cooperatives turn against their weakest members, insurance companies avoid the risks they should insure, and organizations for giving aid to others are often best at caring for themselves.

In the Established Model it is said that the productivity of organizations cannot be significantly improved if they are labor-intensive. In other words, when organizations cannot get rid of us by displacing us with machines, flunking us out, or killing us off, there can only be piddling gains in organizational productivity. By and large, the National Commission on Productivity and Work Quality speaks for such perceptions of the Established Model and focuses on efficiency in producing things.[2]

When research in some field of science becomes unproductive, a new perception model is sought to open doors to further progress. No ideas or processes now exist in the Established Perception Model for improving the productivity of service organizations except by displacing people—as we can easily see and as leading speakers for the system tell us. Inexorably, if we are to be served instead of injured, we must shift to Target Model perceptions and processes for improving productivity in service organizations. (See Figure 12-1.)

People

People are important—not in the Established Model, where they are exposed as inferior machines, but in the Target Model, where they are revealed as competent beings who combine such attributes as the devotion of dogs, the intelligence of dolphins, the inquisitive friendliness of chickadees, and the responsibility of stotting gazelles. If people are inferior to machines in stamping things out with cold, precise repetition, so then are machines inferior to people in creating, nurturing, supporting, responding, caring, sharing, developing, and improving, which are the functions of organizations that serve people.

FIGURE 12-1
Schistosomiasis

All the patterns of perception and organization that appeared in earlier chapters can be related to control of this disease.

An estimated 300 million people are now infected with schistosomiasis, slowly being debilitated by this horrible disease. Its victims are poor rural people living in underdeveloped countries, which may be why so many of us have never heard about it. And unlike malaria, it does not readily spread to the urban rich, which may be why so little effort has been made to control it. A significant part of the present worldwide research effort against the disease is being carried out by the Research and Control Center in St. Lucia on an annual budget of less than half the salary of the president of General Motors.

The Center was jointly sponsored to test control measures by The Rockefeller Foundation, the British Medical Council, and the government of St. Lucia. I visited it in my capacity as comptroller of the Foundation. There I saw the daily activities that make up the visible part of field research—seemingly simple things like making stool examinations or running a plastic pipe to provide a few fresh water faucets in a village.

Infected snails in irrigation ditches and streams release organisms which bore into the body of those who come in contact with the water. Inside a human body the organisms metamorphose into worms, which then start laying eggs. The worm pairs may accumulate in a specific vital organ, impairing function until, after a number of years, the organ is seriously damaged and perhaps the victim dies. Throughout the course of the disease, however, most of the eggs are excreted with the victim's stools. In water the eggs hatch into organisms which infect snails to start the cycle anew.

How to break the cycle? On a test basis chemotherapy has been used to kill worms in human bodies, molluscicides have been used to kill snails, and pure water lines have been provided so people can wash themselves and their clothes without going into infected streams. Success is limited when only one control method is used, and costs increase when the methods are used in combination. Someday, it is hoped, there will be a vaccine, and the Foundation is sponsoring immunological research elsewhere. But isn't education always the best answer? Why not teach school children where to defecate?

Well, I visited a rural school with a thousand students and went into a big room where over four hundred of the younger children sat on benches. Sparkling eyes, clean clothes, beautiful, bright, friendly. And I learned that in the last decade the school had been modernized by installing a few toilets. But there was still no money for toilet paper so they wiped themselves with their hands and their hands on the walls. There was no water in the school and an infected stream across the road was the nearest place to rinse hands, wash out lunch containers, and quench thirst. Health education is not much help under such circumstances.

It appears that the control of schistosomiasis will develop into an organizational problem from a scientific one. The great and dedicated scientific work of the staff at the Research and Control Center and of scientists elsewhere deserves to be followed by great organizational work, both governmental and private. It is hard to conceive, however, that the methods of the Established Model can effectively serve the people they exclude, whether those people are in the ghetto of an industrial city or the rural areas of an underdeveloped country. The effective delivery of health services, as we have seen, must involve the consumer as a producer, and that is done at the Fusion level in the Target Model.

Target Model Organizations need people who respect people. My friend Dr. Edward Lewis, who recently retired as Dean of Cooperative Education at Manhattan Community College, told of an early experience. He was working in the Urban League in Missouri and he received a call from the director of a home for boys, mostly black and delinquent. "Come on over tomorrow, Ed, because there will be a county judge here you should meet. Some people think he isn't much, but I don't agree. He is one board member who visits the home and talks with the boys." And that was how Ed Lewis met Harry Truman. Both men had distinguished and productive careers because they perceived *us* with respect in the Target Model, not *them* with disdain in the Established one.

Processes

Processes are important. As a specific, they induce or reverse senility. As a generality, they induce or reverse all developing and achieving in individuals and organizations. But processes must be perceived before they are seen. Without perception models for celestial processes, the ancients personalized and deified the sun and moon and paid them homage. Beset by dark days, storms, and accidents, and without a perception model for the processes of distortion and withdrawal, attendants and oldsters in nursing homes also personalize their problems, bully, placate, or appease, listen for moods, hope for little courtesies, pray for respites, submit. To improve things, we must change people problems into work processes. Our problems become unsolvable when we personalize or deify.

The structure of an organization is defined by its charter, by-laws, governance plan, organization chart or chain of command, and job descriptions. The drafters and readers of these documents, if they have no perception of Target Model processes, see only a hierarchical pyramid of authority which has no place for the consumer as a producer. Without a Target Model atop the hierarchy, however, an organization is not structured to respond and serve. Organizational productivity for people is derived from Target Model processes.

WHAT'S AHEAD

Service organizations have become important and will remain important. If they remain in the Established Model, the scenario is already clear. If they are made into Complete Organizations with both Established and Target Models, there will be a different scenario.

The Established Model Scenario

An increasing percentage of the population will be excluded from the system. The excluded individuals, already one in three, will act with indifference, hostility, and violence. They will loiter, litter, vandalize, defile, rip off, burglarize, and mug. Individuals within the system will double-lock their doors at home, submit to airport searches, and seek in vain for safety. Individuals and corporations will move from urban to suburban areas. They will try to afford private academies instead of public schools, private cars instead of public transportation, and will leave cities, schools, buses, and subways to those they deplore and fear.

Organizations will get bigger and more impersonal, because Authority is rated by how far it reaches and how strongly. To improve ratings in an Established Model Organization, Authority must be exercised over increasing numbers of people in more and more aspects of their lives. To enhance the strength of Authority as its range extends, it must be administered with increasing uniformity of directives, rules, laws, and impersonal standards. Diversity, exceptions, and responsiveness to the unique needs of individuals are incompatible with the Established Model. The domination of the federal government will grow. Since the exercise of Authority substitutes compliance for responsibility and morality, lying will become recognized as normal, with the highest government officials including presidents already having acknowledged that they lie to serve the system and themselves. Bribery of government officials at home and abroad has already been stated to be an integral part of the system by chief executives of major corporations; their companies reward them for their crimes. No one will have credibility.

The inversion of procedure and purpose will accelerate. More regulatory agencies will be controlled by the industries they are supposed to regulate. Ethics committees of professional societies will strengthen the protection of their members from the public. Military intelligence has already been falsified for political purposes and thousands of soldiers in Vietnam have died because the truth was withheld from military commanders. Spying, wiretapping, blackmail, murder, and assassination have already been seen as practices of governments at all levels, usually by the very agencies that we set up to protect us from such crimes. No human right or freedom will withstand the inversions.

With trust destroyed, things that are true and valid will be impossible to distinguish from things that are false and invalid. At the moment of this writing, there is a tested inexpensive additive which could reduce the use of fossil oil in the United States by 10 percent or more. It improves mileage in cars, reduces fuel consumption in home heating, lessens pollution, and greatly reduces engine maintenance requirements. The additive was developed by an individual inventor. My friends Bob McConnell, now deceased, and his son Frank helped finance the public corporation in Canada which built the first production plant. There have been sales to a school system here and a trucking firm there, but no major sales. Who in big government or big business could believe or be better off for believing that the additive might work? In the Established Model, people and integrity are rejected, not respected—and productivity will not improve.

The Target Model Scenario

There will be obnoxious tension. Two hundred years ago the United States of America was launched as a Complete Organization with a strong Target Model. Its Declaration of Independence, asserting respect for individuals, provoked a revolution. Its Constitution, defining coordinate roles instead of hierarchical authority, provoked confrontations, tests, feedback, and amendments. The government was planned to fit people and their needs. Then, with dramatic advances in material well-being resulting from the Industrial and Scientific Revolutions, management in the Established Model asserted that people must serve the system and must alter themselves or be altered to fit its needs. The power and the glory of the Target Model was gone. Now people are important again, at least in service organizations, and reinstating the Target Model will provoke obnoxious tension.

There will be roles and expectations for people. Creating and maintaining roles will be a function of effectiveness in the Target Model just as eliminating jobs is a function of efficiency in the Established Model. There will be more payments for filling roles, such as stipends to students and artists, and fewer payments for welfare or charity.

The power of individuals and small diverse organizations will be welcomed instead of feared, scorned, and suppressed. Peer counseling will be widely used for training in Target Model processes. Small farmers will be aided throughout the world because they are essential to progress in the program for conquest of hunger. Buildings, equipment, and furnishings will be remodeled and repaired instead of leveled, scrapped, and replaced with uniform modules. The size of organizations will be determined by their roles instead of by the appetite and technology of Authority.[3]

> Once that first summer she said her goal was to do the little things nicely—and I only partly understood. As the years went by the little things accumulated. Each feeding of the babies, each purchase of a toy, each preparing of a meal, each ironing of clothes. Each care and caring in the family, each patient need when she went back to nursing. Each course she took, each student when she started teaching. Each lesson, each question, each grade. Unrelenting, unwavering, unsparing of herself, she lives her process and her process transcends all else I have seen.

Processes of the Target Model will make the elements of psychic reward practical, namely, having one's own goals, own methods, and feedback.[4] Care and craftsmanship will be appreciated in individuals, rehabilitation teams, and organizations. Developing will be more important than exploiting. Achieving will displace defeating and rejecting as the goal. The work ethic will be rediscovered where it was left in the Target Model.

The Question from Chapter Nine

Why should we strive for more productivity and more individual achievement in a world that already has more of them than top managers can manage? Because they are needed in the Target Model. The Established Model describes its limited capacity for productivity and individual achievement in many ways, such as: the control span of executives, the set speed of assembly lines, and various applications of Pareto's law. Conversely, the Target Model builds on strengths and virtues the Established Model rejects: responsibility, initiative, and creativeness, to name a few.

Why should we strive for more productivity and more individual achievement in a world that already has more of them than top managers in the Established Model can manage? It is not the answer that is hard to come by, but the question, and the understanding that the questioning is relevant and valid. Without the questioning, established ways continue and our future will be shaped by our assumptions. What's ahead for us? Only what our ways and processes lead us to.

DEVELOPING THE FUTURE

We have seen that the discoveries of scientists are predetermined by their perceptions and their methods. Looking through microscopes, for example, is obviously not the way to discover a new star or planet. By the same logic, the future scenarios for organizations are predetermined by our perceptions, measurements, and methods. With vocabularies and journals that communicate only Established Model perceptions, and with schools of business that teach only Established Model methods, we obviously are not on the way to a Target Model scenario.

Critical Mass

An individual can react effectively to the system, but it takes more than one to change it. More than one is needed for arriving at consensus, coordinating, accepting, and including. More than one is needed for closing the feedback loop. The minimum number needed to change the system and sustain the change can be referred to as the *critical mass,* a term borrowed from physical science, where it refers to the minimum mass needed to sustain a nuclear chain reaction.

In human affairs, the usual term for critical mass is a *school*: "a group of persons whose thought, work or style demonstrates some common influence or unifying belief."[5] Thus we have schools of art in which special styles develop. And in science, Thomas S. Kuhn tells us, there is the scientific group which shares a paradigm. "When the individual scientist can take a paradigm for granted he need no longer, in his major works, attempt to build his field anew, starting from first principles and justifying the use of each concept introduced. That can be left to the writer of textbooks. Given a textbook, however, the creative scientist can begin his research where it leaves off."[6]

We need a graduate school of productivity for service organizations which will do teaching and research at the Target Model level. Accounting, for example, is now being taught as "the language of business" in the Established Model, with techniques like standard costs and exception reports for enforcing Authority. Auditing is now being taught as a method of control and not as a review process which assists in Developing. Personnel management is now being taught in terms of ranking and rejecting, or at the Influence level. Economics is now being taught in terms of pseudomeasurements of productivity by treating capital depletion (depletion of natural resources) as income. Finance is now being taught and practiced in the context of those large organizations which have access to stock and bond markets, leaving small businesses and private nonprofit organizations to their own shoestrings or to support by government agencies. But government agencies and governments themselves are without the accounting, auditing, personnel, and financial concepts at the Target Model level which would enable them to function effectively.

Within each process of the Target Model there is research to be done and textbooks to be written. The vital interactions between the Target and Established Models in a Complete Organization call for research and exposition. But the research being done today in business schools is almost exclusively for the Established Model alone. We need a graduate school of productivity for the Target Model.

FIGURE 12-2
Threshold Events

Sequence of scientific development from description of structure, to classifications, to measurements, to causes and effects, to complex processes, to threshold events.

Early geomorphologists described mountains, valleys, rivers and hillsides and then they classified them. Later geomorphologists used mathematical equations to describe and classify more precisely. Then their knowledge of structure led them to questions of causes and effects. What caused the remarkably equal spacing of desert sand dunes? Why do rivers always seem to assume a uniformly shaped profile?

Investigation of causes and effects started in terms of simple relationships like an input A leading to an output B and then to measurements like equations to describe the erosive action of flowing water. By stringing causes and effects in sequence, theories were developed. One theory for fluvial phenomena held that rapid mountain building produced steep topography drained by energetic rivers. Through time the topography was eroded, thereby reducing stream gradients and also the energy available for further erosion. Eventually the river gradients became so gentle that further work of erosion was almost impossible unless, of course, there was a new episode of mountain building. The systems framework of this model can be described as closed; there are clearly defined boundaries across which no import or export of materials or energy takes place.

Geomorphologists then became intrigued by the remarkable stability of systems, like river systems, and their capacity for self-regulation as a consequence of complex feedback mechanisms. The older studies had showed that decreases in a river's gradient were caused by a process change, namely a gradual decrease in the river's ability to erode by its inherent velocity. The newer more complex studies showed that in turn gradient controls velocity. An important corollary to the circular process-response approach in geomorphology is the new recognition of a threshold phenomenon. Rivers tend toward equilibrium states in which fluctuations of properties such as gradient are balanced about a constantly changing average condition. The balance can be upset, however, by a threshold phenomenon. Catastrophic floods are examples of river processes that may exceed a threshold of resistance to change and thereby create a whole new equilibrium state in a river system. Current research on rivers is attempting to analyze these thresholds.

Source: Personal correspondence from V. R. Baker, Ph.D., to the author.

> Do you happen to be familiar with Chris Argyris' argument that even those of us who profess your "Target Model" have had such powerful conditioning in the established organizational model that our habitual behavior contradicts the progressive theories we espouse? Hence, experimental schools fail, not because the theories they proclaim are fallacious, but because administrators, teachers, parents and children fall back on customary patterns of control which contradict our alleged ideals. It seems to me an important issue and when you prepare your book you may well want to discuss it.[7]

Minicultures at the Target Model level are continually emerging all around us: an athletic team, an office, a family, an International Rice Research Institute, a school, a club, a tenants' association, a cooperative. Some of them become Complete Organizations and survive a while before they regress to the Established Model under pressure from a society that acknowledges only Force, Authority, and Influence. Young parents, seeking something better for their children than Force, Authority, and Influence, but unaware of the next steps in the Hierarchy of Methods, perceive permissiveness as the only alternative. Permissiveness, however, means relinquishing parental responsibilities and roles and excludes both parents and children from the Target Model. We need a school and textbooks to snowball the knowledge that society as a whole, as well as its component families, businesses, and nonprofit organizations, need not be analogues for zoos.

Threshold Moment (See Figure 12-2)

Today we must pay for costs deferred from yesterday: unacknowledged costs like pollution, hidden costs like neglected maintenance, unmeasured costs like those for federal pensions. Today we must protect ourselves from many people: excluded multitudes that overflow the ghettos, people whose hands are all the system deals with, friends and associates who try to make us lose so they can win. Today we must suffer attitudes and values that the system's processes have introjected into us and others: indifference, intolerance, animus, fear, and violent righteousness, to name a few.

Within limits a system maintains dynamic balance and stability. Prices are raised to reduce demand for scarce supplies. Crises are met by more rejecting and excluding—more layoffs and more forced retirements. Financial credit is provided for consumption today in exchange for repayment tomorrow—as long as tomorrow is credible. But the Established Model has passed three landmarks as it compensates, adjusts, and balances: (1) more than one-third of the population is now excluded from the system, (2) more than one-third of the jobs are in service organizations where the system cannot work, and (3) more than one-third of the gross national product is spent by governments where the measurements and values of the system do not apply. We need a Target Model.

The Established Model can survive alone if we change the world to fit it by burning books, destroying values, and eliminating outside people. By 1984 we can have our Hitler here, our Warsaw ghetto, and our Hiroshima. Now is another threshold moment. Our world is overflowing the Established Model and we must add a Target Model or blot the outside out.

CONCLUDING ABSTRACT

The book has presented a taxonomy of organization methods and has related those methods to the results they can achieve. It has distinguished sharply between the methods which are efficient for physical production and those which are effective for rendering services to people.

Since measurements as well as methods control results, several new approaches to measuring organizational productivity were presented. In addition, patterns for perception of underlying realities were described and illustrated. The use of methods, measurements, and perception models to improve organizational productivity was set forth in manual style.

In service organizations the roles of people are essential, and the book explained why this is so. It went on to discuss the reciprocal patterns of organizational methods and individual reactions. Conversely, it presented the reciprocal patterns of individual actions and organizational reactions. It analyzed why individuals need organizations and how they can best act in relation to them.

It suggested that some major social problems are the result of using inadequate perception models, inappropriate measurements, and wrong-level methods. What might be done to achieve a "critical mass" of adequate perception models, appropriate measurements, and right-level methods was set forth.

NOTES

[1] Statistics comparing the importance of service organizations in 1900 and in the 1970s were taken from a number of sources, including: *The 1975 U.S. Factbook, The American Almanac,* Grosset & Dunlap, Inc., New York; Herman E. Kross, *American Economic Development,* Prentice-Hall, Inc., Englewood Cliffs, N.J., 1974; *Changing Times,* October 1975; and Selig Greenberg, *The Quality of Mercy,* Atheneum Publishers, New York, 1971.

[2] *Fourth Annual Report,* National Commission on Productivity and Work Quality, Washington, D.C., 1975.

[3] E. F. Schumacher, *Small Is Beautiful,* Harper & Row, Publishers, Incorporated, New York, 1973, p. 61.

[4] The three elements of psychic reward were stated by Goodwin Watson at a colloquium of Union Graduate School in January 1974.

[5] *The American Heritage Dictionary,* American Heritage Publishing Co., Inc., New York, and Houghton Mifflin Company, Boston, 1969.

[6] Thomas S. Kuhn, *Structure of Scientific Revolutions.* The University of Chicago Press, Chicago, 1962, p. 19.

[7] The reference to Chris Argyris is taken from a letter by Goodwin Watson to the author. Argyris develops his theories in *Executive Leadership,* Harper & Brothers, New York, 1953; *Personality and Organization,* Harper & Row, Publishers, Incorporated, New York, 1957; *Integrating the Individual and the Organization,* John Wiley & Sons, Inc., New York, 1964; *Intervention Theory and Method,* Addison-Wesley Publishing Company, Inc., Reading, Mass., 1970; and *The Applicability of Organizational Sociology,* Cambridge University Press, New York, 1974.

Index